SET FREE FROM ME

SET FREE FROM ME

by

Paula Russell

Cover design by Endtime Computer Graphics.

Spiritual Hospital Publications
941 Central Avenue
Newport, Kentucky 41071

ISBN 0-9762825-0-X

For Worldwide Distribution
Printed in the U.S.A.

ACKNOWLEDGMENTS

I'm grateful to so many who have made significant contributions to this book in ways that only God can know and reward. I trust Him to do just that.

My special thanks go to:

My husband and children for loving me through the painful years of perfectionism.

Alicia, Cole, Jesse, Brooke, Hope, Hunter, and Dane for sharing your "play" time.

Susan for your insight, your wisdom, and your ceaseless dedication to excellence and integrity throughout the editing process.

Pastor John Stevenson for your spiritual covering and practical advice.

The members and leadership of New Hope Christian Center for your encouragement and for your prayers.

The "Golden Shovels" for helping me to realize that I have something worthwhile to say.

Dedication

To my Loving Heavenly Father whose faithfulness, patience, kindness, mercy, and unfailing love have inspired me to seek and find more of You and Your Truth. There are no words to express my gratitude.

To the doctors, nurses, orderlies, and prayer warriors who serve so faithfully to make the Spiritual Hospital a safe place for the hurting to find shelter, spiritual food, and the Savior's love.

To all the wounded healers who have been set free to serve and to give God the glory. This is for you!

Contents

INTRODUCTION

Have you ever contemplated running away from home, but didn't know where to go?

Have you resorted to pills, alcohol, or some equally destructive behavior as a form of escape?

Or have you settled for yet another sleepless night and a tear-stained pillow as a testimony to your pain and emotional torment?

If your answer to any of these questions is "Yes," your Heavenly Father wants you to know that He has seen your tears, heard your prayers, and felt your pain. He wants you to know that you don't have to continue to live the way you're living.

Jesus came to heal the broken-hearted, to set the captives free, and to release those who are in any kind of bondage. Somehow this true, total healing is escaping many sons and daughters in the Body of Christ. It is to this very Body -- the Church -- that those who are hurting and broken should be able to come for the healing they so desperately need, but we can't impart something we don't have or take someone to a place we've never been.

So what's wrong? Why aren't we walking in this truth?

Having experienced the tears and pain of years in ministry struggling to find a place of peace in the midst of the tremendous challenges and the emotional heartbreak of dealing with wounded, hurting people, I found myself broken and in despair. My mind, my emotions, and my body were so weary that I finally cried, "Lord, if You don't do something, if You don't show me something, if there isn't a dramatic change, I just can't go on. It's too hard. It's too heart-breaking. It's too painful." I heard His voice speaking very clearly in my spirit, "If you are finally at the end of yourself, I can help you. If you want to see truth, I will show you. I will help you to understand why you're not yet free." He then led me into a time of prayer and fasting where He exposed the lies I had been believing, some since childhood. He revealed my unhealed hurts and the deceitfulness of my own heart as the true sources of my pain.

The illumination I've received in being "set free from me" has given me a sense of excitement and anticipation I've never experienced. Enjoying Our Lord's sweet presence and yielding to the Holy Spirit as my constant companion and Friend is bringing the deep inner peace and unspeakable joy I've always longed to know.

Because of His great love for you, our Heavenly Father has led me to share with you His revelation of a healing process that will not simply mask your pain, but set you free from everything that hinders you from being all that you were created to be.

Every member of the Body of Christ is called to minister healing to those in need, but there have been some very real obstacles to overcome. Many of us are so consumed with our own pain and the daily strain of keeping our own lives together, juggling work and family obligations, that we have little or no energy left for effectively serving the Savior or ministering to anyone else, and it shows.

Another harsh reality is that "hurting people hurt people," so ministry to them exposes you to pain such as misunderstanding, rejection, and offense. God wants us to see ministering to other individuals and their problems as part of His purpose for us rather than as a source of pain. The truth is that this is next to impossible until we are free from our own pain and woundedness.

When the woman in Matthew 26:7-13 poured all of her precious ointment on the head of Jesus, He explained to His disciples that in that single act of love she was preparing His body for burial. Now in these last days He desires that we once again pour the healing oil, this time upon His Body, the Church, in order to prepare for His return. Just as the woman poured the oil and perfume upon Jesus' head, we are to minister His healing truth and love to his wounded sons and daughters.

Church culture has too long pressured us to deny or to hide our pain, insisting that the answer is to "Get over it!," "Let it go," or "Give it to God." This can rarely be done without a helping hand when the pain is so real and the effects of it have taken such a toll spiritually, mentally, emotionally, and physically. God wants you to experience your breakthrough by literally "going through" while holding His hand. Breakthrough comes from *going* through, from continuing on through pain until you break through to a new level of spiritual understanding and authority. Once you reach that new level, you will never again be defeated and unable to stand in the face of painful circumstances.

My belief is that the end time deliverer will not be one man as Moses was to Israel, but one Body, the Body of Christ. Right now that Body is weakened because so many who have been called to be mighty warriors are wounded from the battle -- tired, discouraged, hurting, and disillusioned. My prayer is that we, the Church, would receive full deliverance and share the path to freedom with others. My prayer is that we, the Body of Christ, will be set free to walk in our calling and to fulfill our destiny.

You are being prepared, positioned, and anointed for this time, and God is calling you to take your place. A willingness to face truth as the Holy Spirit reveals it is essential for your genuine transformation, though not easy to achieve. I challenge you to give God your undivided attention as you read, and see what He will do. He wants to meet you in the midst of your pain and embrace you with His love so that you will be forever free.

Chapter 1

Reality Check

Have you ever been lost in a mall or in an office building? It's always such a relief to find a map of the building complex to help you find your way. But even when you know the place you're trying to find and you locate it on the map, you must also look for that little marker that says *You Are Here* in order to reach your destination.

When you ask God to help you find your place of peace, He must first show you exactly where you are and how that relates to where He wants you to be. As God speaks to you, His revelation will be true at every level. It will be true in the natural, in the spiritual, and in the realm of your soul. If you are truly seeking Him as you read these pages, His healing word will come and accomplish an awesome work that will be seen in your body, your home, your church, and your ministry.

Discovering where you are is only the beginning of a unique spiritual journey. This journey will take you from living your life with a sense of being overwhelmed, depressed, overworked, confused, and bitter to a place of peace. You will enter a new dimension of the presence and the power of God in your life. Even if you are experiencing a sense of desperation and separation from God right now, you are in a good place.

Finding out where you are involves examining what you do, why you do what you do, and what weaknesses and vulnerabilities are working against you. Our nature is to hide from God when we do something wrong or if we know we are in a negative frame of mind. We read in Genesis 3:9-10:

> *"Then the Lord God called to the man, and said to him, 'Where are you?' And he said 'I heard the sound of Thee in the garden, and I was afraid because I was naked; so I hid myself.'"*

If Adam had only run *toward* God instead of hiding *from* Him things might have been amazingly different for us right now. The truth is that God knew exactly where Adam was, both physically and spiritually, but He wanted Adam to stop and take a look at where he was and what he had done. He is asking you to do the same thing.

God never asks a question to gain information – He is all-knowing. He asks in order to allow us to see where we are so that we can be set free. I've found out the hard way that when I hide myself from God, I end up losing myself and a vital part of my identity. Matthew 16:26 asks:

> *"For what will a man be profited, if he gains the whole world, and loses his soul? Or what will a man give in exchange for his soul?"*

If we will be honest with ourselves, many Christians, even those in ministry, are often uncomfortable in the presence of their Heavenly Father. It's easier to keep working, ministering, and trying to fill the void with busyness than to stop, turn toward Him, and say, "God, this isn't working. I need your help. I need your truth. I need to be set free and made whole." Sadly, though, until we have exhausted all other resources, we rarely choose to approach the only One who has the answers and the authority we need. Hebrews 4:16 encourages us with *"Let us therefore draw near with confidence to the throne of grace, that we may receive mercy and find grace to help us in our time of need."* Then in John 6:68 we read, *"Simon Peter answered Him, "Lord, to whom shall we go? You have the words of eternal life."*

If no one else has the answers we need, why do we fight going to Him? Because true communication with God requires a level of intimacy and honesty that many of us have not yet achieved. But the Word of God reveals His desire for our relationship in Matthew 11:28: *"Come to Me, all who are weary and heavy-laden, and I will give you rest."*

Past hurts really do affect how you relate to others and to God. Sometimes a failed relationship, a huge disappointment, or a betrayal will cause you to put up so many walls and defenses that you can't even let God in. You need to allow yourself to be drawn into a closer, more personal relationship with the Lord. If you do, and if you choose to trust God to help you deal with the pain in your heart, it will make a huge difference in your relationships and interactions with people.

If you are not already transparent in the presence of the Lord, that's the next step in finding where you are. You need to pray that your desire to be all that God wants you to be will be stronger than your negative emotions or your fear. Your honesty will not reveal anything He doesn't already know. Pray that your love for Christ will compel you to seek the answers you need not just to go on, but to enjoy the journey.

In Job 6:24 Job prayed: *"O Lord, teach me, and I will be quiet; show me where I have been wrong."* In Job 34:32 he prayed: *"Teach me what I cannot see, O Lord; if I have done wrong, I will not do so again."* Even though he was an extremely prosperous man who had walked uprightly before God his entire life, Job realized that there were certain issues in his life that he hadn't seen clearly. Through his time of testing, as he maintained an honest heart before God, his hidden fears and impure thoughts were revealed.

Most of our motives are hidden deep inside us. Your Heavenly Father wants you to search your heart and allow Him to reveal the things that shouldn't be there. Proverbs 20:5 says, *"A plan in the heart of a man is like deep water, But a man of understanding draws it out."* God wants you to know the truth about why you do the things you do, why you feel the way you feel, why you can't sleep at night, or why you can't trust Him and stand confidently on His Word.

My own search revealed to me some unexpected realities. On the outside, I always appeared to "have it together" and I was the master of what a "pastor's wife" is expected to say and to do in any particular situation. But on the inside I had somehow confused my "role" in ministry with my "identity" as a child of God.

You could also be experiencing an identity crisis if you ever confuse what you do with who you are. You may feel good about what you do and yet not feel good about you. That's why it's so important for you to understand that Jesus loves you for who you are, not for what you do. It is vital to know who you are because over your lifetime your roles may change, but your identity will remain the same. It's dangerous to become too comfortable with any one particular role -- wife, mother, employee, friend. Your roles may change according to God's timing and His purpose for your life, but your identity as His child will never change.

Do you ever feel pulled by the roles people expect you to play in their lives? You may be surrounded by people, with your phone ringing day and night, and still feel alone and unappreciated because there's no real fellowship or relationship beyond "what can you do for them today." After years of struggling and juggling and guilt trips and disappointment because I had failed at being the perfect mom, the perfect teacher, the perfect pastor's wife, the perfect daughter, the perfect wife, the perfect "anything," I simply couldn't take it anymore. When I cried out to God He began to reveal the lies that the enemy had used to keep me from being blessed, even though my life had been a blessing to those I had been trying so hard to please. He revealed the awesome truth that set me free *from* me to be free *for* those who loved and depended upon me.

If you're like me, it's probably beginning to dawn on you that perhaps you are not where you thought you were or exactly where you're supposed to be. That's a starting point. If you're tired of the games, of having to perform, of pretending that everything is okay when your heart is filled with anger, resentment, and bitterness, God can open the door to freedom -- freedom to simply *be* who you really are. If you've come to a time in your life when all the activity and social events you've used to avoid loneliness now leave you feeling more empty than emptiness could ever be, there's a place you can be absolutely alone and never feel the least bit lonely. If you are stuck in a religious rut or on a performance treadmill, God knows how to get you unstuck. He is ready to replace your destructive thought patterns and selfish habits with the mind of Christ and a love for others that will elevate you to a higher level in Him. According to John 10:10: *"The thief comes only to steal, and kill, and destroy; I came that they might have life, and might have it abundantly."*

Your Heavenly Father not only desires to but is well able to heal the pain of your past and to use everything you've been through to establish you and to make you strong. Jesus gave His life so that you could live life to the fullest, walking in confidence rather than constantly struggling with depression, anxiety, and fear.

If you know that God has called you higher than you've gone and to a place deeper in Him than you've experienced, it's not too late to make a change. You may have started out strong saying, "Lord, I won't let You down. I'll seek Your face. I'll put You first." You may have spent some time in prayer, even tried to praise your way through some difficulties, but for some reason you didn't go all the way. You're not alone. "Halfway there" is where a multitude of believers have stalled out. You may be using your pain or your "bad luck" as an excuse for slowing down, but God says, "Your faithfulness to me even through the pain is exactly why I've chosen you. Please don't give up too soon and forfeit your destiny."

There's a true story told about a man who sold everything he had in an East Coast city to travel out West to mine for gold. Years later, tired, disillusioned, and broke, he finally gave up and sold the land he was mining for practically nothing and returned home in defeat. The new owner of his mine had been digging for only three days when he hit a mother lode that made him a millionaire.

You may be like that man, discouraged and maybe even ready to give up. You may already have quit on the inside but you're still "going through the motions." No one knows you've quit, but inside you've abandoned your dreams. You don't want to continue to risk being hurt and disappointed one more time. You had such high hopes, but you've run into so many obstacles and had so many seemingly unanswered prayers that you've decided to adjust your expectations to your perceived limitations and just keep smiling.

Please be encouraged to believe right now. You can't quit! God has too much for you to do! It is what you endure for Him that expresses how deeply you want what He has for you. Your pain is not a punishment – it is a push toward your destiny. Don't allow it to be in vain. God wants to revive your faith and renew your passion! Your breakthrough will come as you trust your Heavenly Father, Your Loving Savior, and the Holy Spirit to lead you through.

Chapter 2

Future Reality

D o you realize what an honor it is to be called by God?

God *has* called you

Psalm 65:4 says, *"Blessed is the man You choose and cause to come near that He may dwell in your courts. We shall be satisfied with the goodness of Your house."* Ephesians 1:4 says, *"just as He chose us in Him before the foundation of the world, that we should be holy and blameless before Him...."* And John 15:16 says, *"You did not choose me, but I chose you."*

Every serious believer experiences this call, this divine urge, this pulling on the heart to get closer to God and to commune with Him. You may have heard Him say, "I want to take you deeper. I want to bring you more revelation and greater discernment. I want to bless you above and beyond your wildest dreams." If you'll be honest, it's not your

27

work, your health, or your family commitments that stress you to the point of missing God's best. Surprisingly, not all who hear His call are willing to respond. But whenever you do yield to His call, even if it's in the middle of the night or interrupting you at work, you'll come from those times with a God-given word that will enable you to walk in greater spiritual authority. No one can spend quality time in the presence of the Lord and not be changed.

"Now" is one of those God-appointed times. Let "now" be a defining moment in your life -- a time when something profound, even life-changing, causes you literally to be transformed by God.

You are designed for your purpose. You are perfect for your purpose. Jeremiah 1:5 tells us, *"Before I formed you in the womb I knew you. And before you were born I consecrated you."* There are almost seven billion people in the world and not one with the same fingerprint or DNA as you. You are the only one uniquely designed for what God has called you to do. That's why you're so valuable to God. That's why the enemy has tried so hard to distract and to discourage you. Think about it.

God uses His Word to complete your transformation into the person He has planned for you to be. Isaiah 55:11 assures us, *"So shall my word be that goes forth out of my mouth. It shall not return unto me void, but it shall accomplish that which I please, and it shall prosper in the thing whereto I sent it."* What God speaks is predestined to prosper and sent out to accomplish a specific purpose.

God knows -- *and loves you* -- as you are

God knows you better than you know yourself. He knows of your successes even before you succeed. He knows of your failures even before you fail. Hebrews 4:13 says, *"And there is no creature hidden from His sight, but all things are open and laid bare to the eyes of Him with whom we have to do."*

His knowledge is all-inclusive, spanning the gaps between time and incidents. He knows your thoughts even as you unconsciously gather them together to make sense of them in your mind. Psalm 139:1-4 says that every thought you think, God already knew when, where, and why you were going to think it:

> *"O Lord, You have searched me and known me. You know when I sit down and when I rise up; You understand my thoughts from afar. You scrutinize my path and my lying down, and you are intimately acquainted with all my ways. Even before there is a word on my tongue, Behold, O Lord, You know it all."*

You have an outer life that everyone sees and an inner life that no one sees but you and God. God is not impressed with the outward things that seem to impress family and friends. He is not even as interested in what you do as in why you do it. What concerns your Heavenly Father is your inner, hidden man of the heart. This is where He must be permitted access in order to bring you to the fulfillment of His call on your life. The flesh must be cut away. The mind, will, and emotions must come to a new level of obedience. The cry of Psalm 139:23-24 will bring help:

"Search me, O God, and know my heart. Test me and know my anxious thoughts. See if there is any wicked way in me and lead me in the way everlasting."

God isn't nearly as concerned with your past as you are. His concern is with where you are now and in bringing you into His Jeremiah 29:11 plan for your future: *"I know the thoughts that I think toward you, says the Lord, thoughts of peace, and not of evil, to give you an expected end."* He wants you to rest in the knowledge that you have a Heavenly Father whose greatest joy is to fulfill the dreams he has placed in your heart.

You may still be struggling to see yourself as absolutely, unconditionally loved by God. You may know His love on an intellectual level, but you don't realize or truly believe with all of your heart that you are accepted by Him just as you are, that you can find tender mercy and healing for the wounds of life and for your bruised heart.

Prayer:

Holy Spirit, comfort me right now.
Bring divine revelation of my Father's love.
In Jesus' Name.

God prepares you through tests and trials

It's so vitally important for you to understand that the circumstances you suffer in life do not mean that God does not love you. Even when the unwelcome situations in which you find yourself are your own doing, God will use those difficult circumstances to strengthen you and to prepare you to fulfill your destiny.

God has seen every tear and trauma you've experienced. He understands your fear of being hurt again. It is not His will for you to live the rest of your life in fear and dread. He wants you to learn to welcome each trial you encounter as a test designed to strengthen you. James 1:2-4 instructs:

> *"Consider it all joy, my brethren, when you encounter various trials, knowing that the testing of your faith produces endurance. And let endurance have its perfect result, that you may be perfect and complete, lacking in nothing."*

Every great man or woman of God has had to come through some type of challenge as a time of teaching and testing. God allowed Joseph to endure loneliness, fear, rejection, persecution, slander, and even the threat of death in order to develop him into a man of maturity, integrity, and humility for a specific time in history. Joseph eventually had an opportunity to get revenge on his brothers, but He had learned through his trials to obey God and to wait for His ultimate purpose to be revealed. Genesis 50:20 records that Joseph told his brothers, *"And as for you, you meant evil against me, but God meant it for good in order to bring about this present result, to preserve many people alive."* Hebrews 5:8 tells us that even Jesus *"Although He was a Son, He learned obedience from the things which He suffered."*

The problems and the rough times you've gone through may actually validate God's call on your life. People who have not been set apart and chosen for a special purpose rarely face serious opposition. When you've made it all the way through your trials, your testimony will be, "I've been where you are. He brought me through, and He'll bring you through, too."

I was recently recalling some of my most painful memories and thinking that some of those circumstances weren't even my fault. There was absolutely nothing I could have done to prevent being hurt. And yet, some of those circumstances *were* my fault, the result of poor choices and selfish decisions. Suddenly, the Holy Spirit interrupted my thoughts with "My child, it doesn't matter if it's your fault or not. You've already been forgiven, and I just want to heal you."

You may not like the situation you're in. You may want to run away or to ignore your problems in hopes they will somehow disappear. But God will turn even the worst nightmare into a testimony of His love and mercy, a gift of grace which is above and beyond what you could even hope or dream. He meant what He said in Romans 8:28: *"And we know that God causes all things to work together for good to those who love God, to those who are called according to His purpose."*

God doesn't use untried merchandise. No matter how difficult your past may have been, God will use even those adversities to prepare you to fulfill your destiny. Testing always precedes promotion, and His testing measure is fire. Everyone who is called by God is either coming from a fire, in a fire, or on their way to a fire. 1 Peter 1:7 explains, *"that the proof of your faith, being more precious than gold which is perishable, even though tested by fire, may be found to result in praise and glory and honor at the revelation of Jesus Christ.*"

He will always require you to do something completely new in order to get you to your next level of blessing.

> If you want to move to a new level of financial blessing, God may instruct you to plant a seed, to look for a new job, or to change your spending habits.

> If you want to move to a new level of health and strength, He may tell you to change your eating habits or to get more exercise.

> If you want to walk in a new level of power and anointing, you will have to spend more time in His presence, maybe even add fasting to some of your prayer time.

> If you want peace instead of chaos in your life, God may require you to pull away from those people who are keeping your life in turmoil.

> If you've been praying for the joy of the Lord to replace your depression and anxiety, He may take you through a time of testing that will teach you the importance of taking your thoughts captive.

You can't expect your life to change if you are unwilling to change. You must be willing to go to a new level of trust and a new level of obedience. Are you ready? I pray that if you choose to continue this journey into truth, you will never be the same again.

Prayer for Finding Truth:

Lord, I know that Your desire is for me to know all truth that has been hidden from me so that I can be set free. (John 8:32)
I acknowledge that there may be areas where I've been deceived by the enemy. (John 8:44)
I thank You for the Blood of Jesus that allows me to be seated with Christ in the heavenlies. (Ephesians 2:6)
Right now, I yield my mind to be conformed to the mind of Christ.
I yield my will to your will, Lord.
Holy Spirit, I yield my spirit to You.
I command all lying and deceiving spirits to loose me now in Jesus' Name.
I ask you, Holy Spirit, to guide me into all truth. (John 16:13)
I ask you to search me, O God, and know my heart. Try me and know my anxious thoughts; and see if there by any hurtful way in me. Lord, lead me in the way everlasting. (Psalm 139:23-24)
I'm ready for you to reveal the things in me that are so deeply rooted, I do not even see them myself. Show me who I really am, what you want me to do, and who you created me to be. (Psalm 139:23-24)
In Jesus' Name.

Chapter 3

Choose Your Pain

We tend to avoid pain at all costs. The reality is that although change can be painful, the consequences of refusing to change are even more painful.

Am I ready to change?

The obvious answer is, "Yes, of course. Why wouldn't I want to change? No one chooses to be nervous, fretful, or in a constant state of fear or anxiety, do they?"

Still, you may not fully understand the pain you may have to go through or how difficult it will be to let go of certain habits and ways of thinking that have become a part of you. Turning your will and your plan completely over to God will bring to a halt the things of the past and take you into God's will for your future. To get in on the abundance of blessings God has for you, you must be willing to allow Him to be in control. The Kingdom of God is just that -- a kingdom -- where Jesus must be permitted to rule and reign.

Be sure that you are not expecting God to bless you *your* way. Change is impossible until you are totally surrendered to *His* way. It may be something seemingly as insignificant as the Holy Spirit prompting you to reconcile with someone when you're not ready, and you won't budge because you are the one who was wronged. You may not think it's right. It may not be fair. But you have to be willing to obey God no matter what. Matthew 5:23-24 instructs us:

> *"If therefore you are presenting your offering at the altar, and there remember that your brother has something against you, leave your offering there before the altar, and go your way; first be reconciled to your brother, and then come and present your offering."*

You may be in a relationship that has been a source of pleasure and fulfillment, but God is forcing some separation and distance between you. You must be willing to leave *when* God says to leave and stay *where* God says to stay. These decisions can be more difficult for you than anyone else could imagine. This is a test of your love for God and of your determination to choose His way.

One of the most challenging changes for me was to stop making excuses or trying to justify my own self-serving actions. When God would question my motives or ask me why I was still doing something He had told me to leave behind, I would find myself rationalizing with, "Yes, I'm disobeying, God, but this is why. You don't understand, Lord. What You are asking is just too hard. It's so much to ask right now while I'm going through all of these other changes. Nobody else is going to that extreme. I'll lose all my friends." Sound familiar? God will never ask you to do anything that is not good for you. He will also never require you to do anything that He won't give you the power to do.

Choose Your Pain

If you'll take a step of faith, God will be there to give you the grace and the provision you need to succeed. Isaiah 30:21 promises: *"and your ears will hear a word behind you. This is the way, walk in it, whenever you turn to the right or to the left."*

There are probably some kind and considerate ways that people in your family or on your job or in your church could make it easier for you to change. I can remember thinking "if my husband would just do this" or "if my work load wasn't so demanding" or "if only this person would be more considerate," but what I'd forgotten was that they're all struggling to find their way and to survive the pressures of life, too. I've found the most peace in praying, "God, while you're working on them, please change *me* first."

Roadblocks on the road to your destiny

Satan knows what God intends for you and he will do anything to keep you from getting there. He knows you have some legitimate needs that are not being met right now, and he is using your pain and frustration to provoke you either to try to fulfill those needs your own way and fall into sin or to give up completely and fail. The Apostle Paul warned us about these subtle devices in II Corinthians 2:11: *"We are not ignorant of his devices."*

On the other hand, self-destructive behaviors and habits can make *you* your own worst enemy. God wants to deliver you from those internal evil tendencies - self-pity, self-righteousness, judgmentalism, anger, unforgiveness, idolatry, envy, loneliness, fear, and rejection, among others - that grieve the Holy Spirit and end up causing pain to you and to those around you.

In the past I blamed my busy schedule, grouchy people, financial problems, or "the church drama of the week" for my lack of peace and joy, but it all eventually boiled down to one nasty common denominator: *me*. My one consolation was in seeing that I was in good company when I read in Paul's letter to the Romans that he had a similar problem. Paraphrasing what he said in Romans 7:19-25: "My new nature loves to do God's will, but there is something deep inside me that struggles against my good intentions. I end up not doing the good I want to do and actually doing things that I know are wrong. My old nature is still warring within me trying to keep me a slave to the sin that is still inside. What am I going to do? Who can free me from myself? Thank God, Jesus has already done it."

Paul understood our very human tendency to live in denial, closing our eyes to the areas of our lives that need to change. Change is hard work, so it's easier to stay as we are. Paul saw past the hardship of the race to the glory of the prize, and that's what we must do, too. Remember, we're in this for life *and* beyond, to eternity. Philippians 3:13-14 exhorts us:

> *"Brethren, I do not regard myself as having laid hold if it yet; but one thing I do: forgetting what lies behind and reaching forward to what lies ahead, I press on toward the goal for the prize of the upward call of God in Christ Jesus."*

Our Wounded Healer

Hebrews 4:15:

> *"For we do not have a high priest who cannot sympathize with our weaknesses, but One who has been tempted in all things as we are, yet without sin."*

Jesus knows how you feel. He hears. He sees. He understands. He is sympathetic toward your situation, but He will not allow you to give in to your feelings because your reaction to those feelings will determine the direction of your life.

Emotional pain is a signal that your soul has been wounded. You may be emotionally bound by childhood trauma or by hurts from years of being taken for granted as you served faithfully in your church or in your home. A wound in your body that is left untreated can become infected and cause serious problems. The same thing happens when your heart becomes wounded through betrayal, rejection, disappointment, or abuse. It affects your emotions causing you to be extremely sensitive. Your pain may manifest in the form of depression, anxiety, irrational fear, or anger, but simply treating the symptoms, whether physical or emotional, won't help. The pressure of suppressing the pain may become so great that it can actually cause you to say and to do things you wouldn't have said or done if you weren't hurting so badly.

You must come to the place where you are ready to ask Jesus to show you the true source of your pain. The good news is that what He reveals, He also heals. Psalm 147:3

says, *"He heals the brokenhearted, and binds up their wounds."* When a wound on your body has healed, there may be a scar, but it is no longer painful. When Jesus heals our heart wounds, the memory no longer throbs with painful thoughts. It no longer yields depression and other destructive emotions. God intends for you not only to be saved and on your way to heaven but to enjoy your life to the fullest. He wants so much to do for you what only He can do and to give to you what only He can give. Jesus said in John 10:10: *"The thief comes only to steal, and kill, and destroy; I came that they might have life, and might have it abundantly."*

For years I ministered to other people not realizing that my driving motivation was to escape feeling my own pain. The pain remained until I allowed the Lord to unmask my "issues" and to help me to deal with them. When you are consumed with your own struggles and most of your time is devoted to escaping your own pain, a huge portion of your available energy is drained from you, leaving you feeling exhausted and barely able to function. If you are unable or unwilling to see the true source of your pain, you may be totally oblivious to the fact that you are not functioning in the freedom, the peace, the joy, and the strength that God intended for you.

God is drawing you to Himself right now. He wants to push you out of your yesterday, to pull you away from your plans for tomorrow, so that He can touch you in a supernatural way in your present situation. To be truly transformed and to make any lasting change, you need to be supernaturally consumed with desire for His presence. He's calling you to total submission and an intimate relationship with Him.

Choose Your Pain

No matter how discouraged you may be or how hopeless your life appears right now, your God has made promises to you and you can't give up without seeing them come to pass. You've got to keep the vision God placed in your heart before you all the way to your "expected end." Don't let Satan steal your dreams. Don't allow anything to keep you from becoming a powerful, joy-filled, victorious Christian example to those watching and following you.

Your decision to change is the open door into God's reality. If you've tried everything and you're still struggling, why not stop and pray, "God, just tell me what to do and I'll do it. Whatever it takes, I'm ready to change." Once you make that decision, heaven will back you up and no one in hell can stop you. You're just one decision away from your journey toward whatever you are believing God for right now.

One word of warning: You will pay a physical and emotional price when you actually become willing to break through your perceived limitations and enter a new area of further potential. Elijah, for example, had found a "comfort zone" by the brook Cherith, so God had to dry up the brook in order to force Elijah to go to the next place where He was needed to minister. If God hadn't stopped the provision, Elijah may never have moved because he was just like you and me: fearful of change. Sometimes God has to use a pink slip, a yellow envelop under the door, or a broken relationship to push you into a new place you've been afraid to go. God wants to change you supernaturally so that He gets the praise. If your dream is within your ability to bring it to pass, it probably isn't big enough.

Once you make the decision to change, look into God's Word as a mirror for change and diligently apply each truth He reveals to you. Guard the entrance of your heart and defend your mind against old thoughts and thought patterns. Be willing to disassociate from the past and remain open to God's correction.

Prayer for Change:

Lord, please change my vision to match Yours.
I choose to cooperate with You to rebuild my life.
Forgive me for the times I have allowed pride, fear of rejection, or dread of another disappointment to keep me from attempting to change.
I know the time is short, and I need You.
Help me to trust the people You have placed in my life to help me.
Give me the courage to let go of the people and things that are holding me back, keeping me separated from You and from Your purpose for my life.
Holy Spirit, help me, comfort me, strengthen me.
In Jesus' Name.

Chapter 4

Who Do You Trust?

Your answer to this question is crucial to where you go from here. Who or what do you trust to be able to heal you and to help you? Who is the first person you call when you're upset or lonely? What is the first thing you do when you or someone in your family is experiencing a crisis?

Believe it or not, many people have trust issues with God. For some, this results from past disappointment or distrust built up by the actions of an earthly father who was never there or who kept making promises and never keeping them. For others, it's the emotional dysfunction that comes from being raised by an authority figure who was impossible to please. Because parents are people too, their human frailties can create distorted images of your Heavenly Father in your heart and mind. You grow up feeling that God sees you and is going to treat you as your parents did. Although it's rarely admitted or discussed, you may hold a subconscious sense that God is like an abusive or an absent parent. Some people actually believe that God is just waiting to judge them or to punish them. In actuality, God is the only perfect parent. You need to believe this about your Heavenly Father in order to trust Him. If you have been threatened and manipulated with a fear of God's wrath as a child, He wants that lie torn down.

Many people place more trust in themselves than in God, but this is definitely not a wise thing to do. The Bible says in Proverbs 28:26: *"He who trusts in his own heart is a fool; but whoever walks wisely, he shall be delivered."* Let's consider this a little more closely:

You can't control your moods.

A few of your relationships are shaky.

You have all kinds of faults and fears.

In this condition, do you really want to hang on to your stronghold of self-reliance?

Or maybe you don't even trust yourself that much. You may have placed your trust in other people, in your bank account, in your job, or in other "modern idols." But when these trusts are broken, strongholds of hurt, disillusionment, resentment, anger, and bitterness are built up. These disappointments further undermine our ability to trust Him because we blame God in order to avoid blaming ourselves or our "idols." The Bible warns us in Isaiah 42:17: *"They shall be turned back and be utterly put to shame, Who trust in idols, Who say to molten images, 'You are our gods.'"*

Only God is fully and unfailingly trustworthy. ·Trusting God yields perfect peace when there is absolute confidence that He will always do what is best. As we are exhorted in Philippians 4:6-7:

Who Do You Trust?

"Be anxious for nothing, but in everything by prayer and supplication with thanksgiving let your requests be made known to God. And the peace of God, which surpasses all comprehension, shall guard your hearts and your minds in Christ Jesus."

Learning to trust Him completely requires that you be willing to lay aside old images and mistaken beliefs about Him. Even if you find something in the Word or hear a teaching that you don't fully understand, trust Him to show you a more complete revelation of that truth.

In what areas of your life do you find yourself trusting in your own strength rather than in God's grace? These are your areas of distrust that God wants to heal.

Prayer:

Lord, I pray for an open mind to see You as You really are.
I pray that Your truth will cause my faith to grow.
Help me to trust You more.
Forgive me for all the times that I've turned to other people or other things for the peace that only You can give.
Help me to really trust You, Lord, with every fiber of my being.
Please fill the empty places within me with Your Presence and help me to rest in Your arms.
Thank You for showing me my weaknesses, my vulnerabilities, the secrets and the needs I didn't even know I had.
I trust You with my future and my fears.
Hold me close and wipe away my tears.
In Jesus' Name.

Chapter 5

Why Is The Word Not Working For Me?

"**S**et Free From Me" was birthed as I labored through my own tears and pain, crying out to God for answers to the questions that burdened my heart. The words "whom the Son sets free is free indeed" kept replaying in my mind. I couldn't understand how I could be a Christian, love Jesus and know Him as my personal Savior, be baptized, Spirit-filled, pray and attend church faithfully, and yet not be walking consistently in the peace, the joy, and the freedom that Jesus died to provide for me.

I struggled with the contrast between the powerful, life-changing effect Jesus and his disciples had upon their world and my feeble attempts to help the hurting men and women in my world. I asked the Lord:

> Why do so many Christians still suffer from depression, anxiety attacks, and physical illness?

> Why is the divorce rate or the number of couples stuck in unhappy marriages just as high among church members and pastors as in the world?

Why are so many of Your people struggling financially, even declaring bankruptcy, when Your Word clearly teaches that Your plan for Your children is blessing and prosperity?

When I had cried until there were no more tears and finally stopped to listen, God spoke. My mind went back to the revival meeting when at only eight years of age I felt the weight of my sin and God's call on my life. I remembered going forward and asking Jesus to come into my heart. I remembered my baptism in the river near our church and how, at the beginning, I was so sure that I knew all about my Jesus. Now, years later, I was acutely aware of the distance between Jesus Christ and me. I was no longer confident in my understanding of Him. I began to see Him as so much more than my mind could comprehend. I was both excited and fearful as He spoke to my spirit, "If you are ready to learn. I will be your teacher."

Wherever you are spiritually right now, God wants to take you to a richer, fuller place of greater understanding. He will take you from the salvation you've known to a deliverance totally out of yourself into a union with Him. John 8:36 promises, *"So if the Son makes you free, you will be free indeed."* It won't be easy, but it is so worth every moment you spend in His presence discovering your Lord and His truth that will, indeed, set you "free indeed."

I Corinthians 2:14 says, *"But a natural man does not accept the things of the Spirit of God; for they are foolishness to him, and he cannot understand them, because they are spiritually appraised."* Reading this scripture with some new insight from the Holy Spirit was a big key to the answer to my questions. Paul is not speaking only of unsaved persons when he speaks of the "natural man." When a person comes to Christ, the spirit is saved but the flesh -- the natural man -- is not. It is that "natural man" who does not want to give up control. This is why one minute you may be a mighty man or woman of God, worshipping with tears of joy streaming down your face, and the next minute you feel like punching someone out.

When you come to Christ, your spirit is saved instantaneously. Acts 2:21 says, *"'And it shall be, that everyone who calls on the name of the Lord shall be saved.'"* You believe it and receive it. It is done. After that, your soul is saved progressively over time as you work out your own salvation and as you are transformed by the renewing of your mind.

> Philippians 2:12-13: *"So then, my beloved, just as you have always obeyed, not as in my presence only, but now much more in my absence, work out your salvation with fear and trembling; for it is God who is at work in you, both to will and to work for His good pleasure."*

> Romans 12:2: *"And do not be conformed to this world, but be transformed by the renewing of your mind, that you may prove what the will of God is, that which is good and acceptable and perfect."*

You must *choose* to work with the Holy Spirit to see to it that what Jesus began in your spirit when you were born again is carried out in your soul and seen in the things you say and do.

It is sometimes extremely difficult to admit *"the real enemy is me."* Once you are saved, you now essentially have two people in one body. Your carnal side and your spirit side are now at war. One part of you loves God and wants to serve Him, while the other side of you loves self and becomes extremely agitated when self doesn't get its way.

Ephesians 6:12 tells us, *"For our struggle is not against flesh and blood, but against the rulers, against the powers, against the world forces of this darkness, against the spiritual forces of wickedness in the heavenly places."* The battle is not in your spirit. Your spirit is born again. The battle is in your flesh.

Think of the challenge of weaning a child. He doesn't want to give up the ease and comfortableness of that bottle. He begins to be fretful, irritable, and might even throw a few temper tantrums. The fretting and anxiety of the flesh is like that child. Most Christians get very upset when you first try to wean them off the *milk* of the Word. They prefer to sit back and be fed. They enjoy attending seminars, conferences, and crusades where teachers, prophets, and evangelists teach the Word with no commitment required. Then they can go home feeling better, but no one holds them accountable for the Word they have heard. No one is there asking them to be faithful, reliable, or dependable. Consequently, all too often, there is no true change. God's Word says in James 1:22:*"But prove yourselves doers of the word, and not merely hearers who delude themselves."*

Many Christians have the mistaken idea that being born again will automatically eliminate all of their emotional hang-ups and personality problems. This is a dangerous misconception. Your mind -- your intellect -- must be renewed with the truth of the Word of God in order for your behavior to be changed. This is a process, not an event. Let's look at a few contrasts between the workings of the spirit and of the flesh.

Your spirit is gentle.	*Your flesh is manipulative and controlling.*
Your spirit yields to God.	*Your flesh demands and dictates.*
Your spirit allows you to be free to do anything that you would not want to hide from God.	*Your flesh makes you feel pressured to do things you would want to hide from God.*
Your spirit is obedient to the Word, willing to wait on God, and full of grace and truth.	*Your flesh is rebellious, impatient, and deceptive.*

Your mind is like the hard drive on a computer. All of your experiences - both good and bad - have been recorded in your memory. They directly and deeply affect your beliefs, your feelings, and your behaviors. They affect the way you look at yourself, your life, your family, and your God.

Make no mistake. Satan wants your mind. One of his favorite strategies is to sow corruptible seeds into your thought processes in order to influence you to adopt his lifestyle and way of thinking rather than to obey and to rely upon the Word of God. You can fight a demonic attack on your mind by using your authority in the Name of Jesus to resist any harmful thought or spirit. You may have a dread or an irrational fear about something because unbelief or a wrong teaching has already been sown into your thinking. Hearing a specific sound or detecting a certain odor may make you extremely uncomfortable or throw you into a negative emotion. This terror or this feeling of discomfort has a very real source. It is most likely coming from an earlier memory or from a hurtful experience in your past. For instance:

> An irrational fear of dentists may have been created in your mind when you had an extremely painful and traumatic experience in the dental chair as a child.

> You may be struggling in your marriage as a result of distrust planted in your mind through a previous experience with the opposite sex.

> You may have a problem with authority figures because someone you should have been able to trust to protect and to care for you was abusive in that role.

Your feelings and emotions are affected when your heart becomes wounded through betrayal, rejection, or disappointment. As previously described, just as a wound in your body can become infected and cause serious problems if left untreated, your wounded heart can become infected with things like guilt, fear, shame, unforgiveness, bitterness, resentment, or rejection. These infections can be extremely painful and even affect your ability to function effectively. They can actually make you "heart-sick" and cause you to say and to do things you would not have said or done if you weren't hurting so badly.

Understanding this will prevent you from judging other people too harshly. This understanding will help you to have patience with people even when their behavior is sometimes confusing and contradictory. You'll realize that they're not fakes, they're not phonies, they're not hypocrites. They're people like you and me with hurts and scars and wrong ways of thinking that interfere with their present behavior. The Bible says in Matthew 7:16, *"By their fruits you shall know them,"* but by their roots you can understand and not judge them.

It is important to realize that we all have certain areas of our lives that need special healing by the Holy Spirit. No matter how much you or your loved one wants to change, no matter how sorry anyone is, no matter how many good intentions anyone has, self-discipline and willpower will never be enough. Long-standing habits of acting and reacting come from severe emotional problems which require transformation from the inside out. You have power through Jesus Christ over the mind of the flesh. He wants to end the tormenting thoughts that are continually causing you pain or causing you to say and to do things that hurt those you love. Romans 8:8 says, *"and those who are in the flesh cannot please God."*

Take a moment and reflect upon the fact that Jesus Christ gave up everything so that you could have everything. He cares about the fact that you are in a physical or emotional prison. For several months a few years ago, I would wake in the middle of the night so agitated that I couldn't even stand being in my own house. I had the mistaken idea that if I went somewhere, anywhere, I could escape the terrible fear and dread and the overwhelming sense of despair I was experiencing. Almost every night was painfully predictable. If the enemy has done that to me, he may try it on you. Jesus paid the price for you to be free. The Cross purchased your freedom from every sin and from every type of bondage and sickness and replaced them with Christ Himself. Jesus is the fulfillment of Isaiah 61:1-4:

> *"The Spirit of the Lord God is upon me, Because the Lord has anointed me To bring good news to the afflicted; He has sent me to bind up the brokenhearted, To proclaim liberty to captives, And freedom to prisoners; To proclaim the favorable year of the Lord, And the day of vengeance of our God; To comfort all who mourn, To grant those who mourn in Zion, Giving them a garland instead of ashes, The oil of gladness instead of mourning, The mantle of praise instead of a spirit of fainting. So they will be called oaks of righteousness, The planting of the Lord, that He may be glorified. Then they will rebuild the ancient ruins, They will raise up the former devastations, And they will repair the ruined cities, The desolations of many generations."*

When Jesus read from this passage He claimed that He was the One empowered by the Holy Spirit to do these things. He wants you to know that these words apply to you in your situation right here, right now, just as they once did for the Israelites. He is telling you, "My child, when you come to Me, nothing can hold you captive." If you've asked Jesus to come into your life, to forgive your sins and to be your Lord, don't go back into slavery to anyone or anything. Christ came to set you free, no matter what type of bondage you're in. No matter what or who broke *your* heart, Jesus came to bind up the broken-hearted.

Why Is the Word Not Working For Me?

A baby elephant born in captivity is tied to a stake as soon as possible to teach him that he can only go as far as the length of the tether or chain. He soon learns that he is captive to that restraint. Then when the elephant is fully grown and could easily pull that little stake and chain right out of the ground, he doesn't even try. He is deceived and is so used to being held to those limitations that he doesn't even test his strength or attempt to escape. You need to see that your only limitations, like the elephant, are in your perception of them. The freedom of your Christian life will be no more and no less than you truly want it to be. Now the choice is yours.

Chapter 6

Exposing the Lies

Many believers discover that their biggest adversary is the spirit of deception. What is deception, anyway? The Greek word for deception – *planos* -- means to be misled or to be led astray and seduced.

From the time you took your first breath of air, the devil has been subtly trying to molest your soul through deception. The reason for his persistence is that He knows that the best way to hurt God, the Creator, whom he hates, is to hurt God's children. He knows that your Father in Heaven has a good plan for your life, a plan with purpose and a divine destiny, and he doesn't want you to find it. But Jeremiah 29:11-13 assures you:

> *"'For I know the plans that I have for you,' declares the Lord, 'plans for welfare and not for calamity to give you a future and a hope. Then you will call upon Me and come and pray to Me, and I will listen to you. And you will seek Me and find Me, when you search for Me with all your heart.'"*

God wants you to experience His power and His glory. It wasn't hard for God to prepare the plan for your life, to prepare a special place of significance in this world for you. What's taking so long is preparing *you*. Arriving at your place of destiny or extreme blessing before you are properly prepared, though, could destroy you. You must allow God to expose the deceptions and beliefs that are based on your wounds, your rejections, and your failures rather than on His Word of truth. In order to be powerful in the Lord you must be teachable and open to correction. You must be willing to do whatever God says to do and to go wherever God says to go.

The Spirit of the Lord is saying to you even as you are reading this book, "I am able to repair your broken places." In order for Him to do that you must allow Him to expose where those broken places are. I once had to take a teaching position replacing an excellent teacher who had been teaching in a classroom on Friday afternoon and was lying in a funeral home by Saturday evening. She died from "walking pneumonia" because she did not realize the severity of her illness and failed to get the proper treatment. In a similar way, you may be walking around broken and bleeding in your spirit, not even knowing what's wrong. All you may know is that you're hurting and that nothing you do quite satisfies you or totally takes away the pain.

Few people are aware that they are constantly being influenced by what other people say or by thoughts planted in their minds by the devil. You may be led away from the truth without even knowing it by programs you watch on TV, by the music you listen to, by what you read or see on the internet, by the places you go, or by the people with whom you associate. These things may not seem so important to you at the time, but the truth is that every choice you make is significant. Every choice you make will affect you spiritually, either for good or for evil.

You can be deceived into speaking curses upon yourself and upon your family without even realizing what you are doing. Remember what Jesus said in Matthew 12:36-37?

> *"And I say to you, that every careless word that men shall speak, they shall render account for it in the day of judgment. For by your words you shall be justified, and by your words you shall be condemned."*

Think about the awesome word in Hebrews 11:3: *"By faith we understand that the worlds were prepared by the word of God, so that what is seen was not made out of things which are visible."* You are made in the image of God. That's why your words have creative power, much like your Heavenly Father's words have.

Romans 4:17 says, *"... even God, who gives life to the dead and calls into being that which does not exist."* Think about this for a moment. If your world is framed by your words, then your words are literally "coming attractions" of how your life is going to be. If you knew that what you were speaking were going to happen, would you keep saying the things you now say on a daily basis?

I've learned to pray for the Holy Spirit to help guard my tongue because it's dangerous to speak against yourself, your family, your spouse, or your church. Your only limitations in this life are your perceptions of them and what you speak from your mouth against God's plan for you. You must stop waiting for your situation to line up to your expectations before you praise and speak a blessing. God told Moses, "You tell them 'As truly as I live, as you have spoken in my ears, so will I do. So shall I perform it.'" Numbers 14:27-28 says:

> *"How long shall I bear with this evil congregation who are grumbling against Me? I have heard the complaints of the sons of Israel, which they are making against Me. Say to them, 'As I live,' says the Lord, 'just as you have spoken in My hearing, so I will surely do to you;'"*

I have learned a little secret after thirty-seven years of marriage:

> Women, every man has a king in him and every man has a selfish, foolish little boy in him. The one you talk to is the one who is going to respond to you.

> Men, you can choose to bring out the tender, loving partner and helpmeet or the hostile, angry nag by the words you speak and the way you say them.

> Parents, every child has both a successful contributor and a dismal failure in them. The words you speak to them will determine the potential they live up or down to.

Be very careful! The enemy wants to steal love from your home. Actually, he must deceive you into doing it for him. Selfishness and self-preservation are robbers. The enemy will use your selfishness to make you believe that you are justified in being upset. He will deceive you into thinking that you have a right to do whatever you are doing because someone else did whatever they did. You are operating in selfishness, not love, when all you can see is *you*, how things are affecting *you*, how the situation is hurting *you*, only thinking about what *you* want and what *you* need. Love gives what the other person needs regardless of what *you* think you need.

There is another deception, one more lie you may have believed that needs to be exposed so that you can be set free from brokenness and bondage. This is the lie that your God doesn't care about you and what you are going through.

There may be some circumstances in your life that you don't like right now. Maybe "can't stand" is more like it. If you're anything like me, you've pushed and you've pushed against that thing. You've worked your faith. You've fought it and fought it, and it's still there. You can't fix everything. If you're pushing against something that simply will not move. Maybe it's not going to move.

What God has shown me is that sometimes our faith is perfected even more when things don't change than when they do change. You don't need faith for what you can see or for what you already have. You need faith when no answer has come yet, when life makes no sense, when you can't explain or understand any of it. That's the time for your faith to shine and for God to receive glory as you praise Him through those very circumstances.

We tend to think there is only one good outcome: the one we want. That's because we haven't yet learned to trust completely in our Heavenly Father and His promise to give good and not evil to His children. When you continue to trust God and to act and react according to His Word even though the pain doesn't go away and the story doesn't seem to have a happy ending -- or at least not the one we wanted – your endurance increases. You do have a choice. If you choose to believe the lie that God has forsaken you, you will eventually become bitter, but trusting through the trial will make you better. James 1:12 says, *"Blessed is the man that endures. He shall receive the crown of life, which the Lord has promised to them that love Him."*

The awesome thing is that God will never leave you alone. He will be right there, going through every trial with you, coaching you, teaching you, sometimes even carrying you. The extent of the pain you're experiencing right now could very well be an indicator of the magnitude of His call upon your life. Only your Heavenly Father and fulfillment of His purpose, no matter how painful it may seem right now, truly satisfies. Ask God to show you the hope within the heartache and move on.

Chapter 7

Spiritual Surgery

W e have established that born again believers have essentially two people in one body and they are at war. It is impossible to walk in victory if you haven't learned how to divide spirit and soul so that you can make choices that will win that war. As you learn to recognize the difference between what your regenerated spirit would choose and what your *un*regenerated soul would choose, you will be able to choose consistently to walk in the Spirit rather than fulfilling the lusts of the flesh.

God's Word is the sword that has the ability to separate soul and spirit and the power to regenerate (or *save*) your soul. Hebrews 4:12 says, *"For the word of God is living and active and sharper than any two-edged sword, and piercing as far as the division of soul and spirit, of both joints and marrow, and able to judge the thoughts and intentions of the heart."* Knowing how to separate soul and spirit comes by doing, using, and acting upon the truth you learn from God's Word. Christ has set you free by the power of His Blood and the power of His Spirit in you. Then you must maintain your freedom as you learn to live day by day, hour by hour, and moment by moment in the power of the Spirit rather than under the power of your flesh. Remember, your soul is made up of your mind, your will, and your emotions. Even though your *spirit* is saved, if you are still reasoning through a *mind* that has not been renewed, and if you are still experiencing the intense pain of a wounded heart full of negative *emotions*, you will not be making choices with your *will* that line up with God's will for your life. As you meditate on God's Word and allow it to do spiritual surgery, cutting and separating the lusts of your flesh from the promptings of the Holy Spirit, you will be set free to make godly choices.

Ephesians 6:12 says, *"For our struggle is not against flesh and blood, but against the rulers, against the powers, against the world forces of this darkness, against the spiritual forces of wickedness in the heavenly places."* It should encourage you to know that even though you are fighting spirit beings in this war they are not fighting your spirit. Your spirit is saved and sanctified. All of these evil principalities and powers can only fight you in the realm of your soul. Satan can only function in the realm of your mind and in the realm of your emotions.

To reach maturity as a Christian, your flesh must be brought under the control of your spirit. Your flesh does not want to be denied and will try to regain control in any area of your life where you have a weakness. In order to wage and win this war you will eventually have to say, "I have met the enemy, and it is I." Then you will mature by consistently making decisions that bring your flesh under the control of your spirit through your own choices such as showing patience, giving the benefit of the doubt, or denying yourself the right to selfishness. You can't afford the luxury of fussing, worrying, murmuring and complaining. You must settle within yourself once and for all that your spirit, not your flesh, will be in control.

The first step is to say "No" to your flesh:

"No, you're not going to buy that."
"No, you're not going to eat that."
"No, you're not going to do that."
"You won't do anything until you check with me
because I deny you the right to move independently of
God."

The Mind

Let's look a little deeper. Your mind really is the battleground for your destiny. Romans 8:6-7 says:

"For the mind set on the flesh is death, but the mind set on the Spirit is life and peace, because the mind set on the flesh is hostile toward God; for it does not subject itself to the law of God, for it is not even able to do so;"

As you understand more about how the enemy attacks your mind, you will know how to stop him. Your mind -- the intellect part of your soul -- must be renewed with the truth of the Word of God so that your behavior can be transformed. The more of God's truth you *experience*, and the more you understand the heart of God, the sooner your mind will be free to do His will. John 8:32 says, *"and you shall know the truth, and the truth shall make you free."*

If you don't submit control of your mind to God, it may go out of control and cause you to do ridiculous things. People always say, "The devil is a liar." So if we know that, why do we listen to him? James 4:7 says, *"Submit therefore to*

God. Resist the devil and he will flee from you." When you submit your mind to the Word of God, you are submitting to God. You must stay on the alert against outside influences such as words from the people in your life or music that brings certain thoughts to your mind. Wrong thoughts bring wrong beliefs. These lead you into wrong reasoning that results in wrong behavior.

If you've been struggling with depression, go back and retrace your thoughts. What have you been thinking about yourself? What have you been thinking about your life, your relationships, your job? Your head may be saying, "This is stupid. Nobody cares what you're doing anyway. You're not going to make it. You may as well give up." When the devil is pounding on your mind, close your eyes for just a minute and say, "Lord, I know you are with me. I am listening to you and I'm going to press through my reaction to these thoughts." Get alone, get quiet, and ask, "Lord, what do You say about this?" The moment a harmful thought comes, take it to God's Word and compare notes. Decide whose report you are going to believe. Learn to be sensitive to the Holy Spirit. Develop the habit of stopping, quieting your soul, and listening to the still, small voice in your spirit. His voice will come from within.

There is an extremely strong tie between thought and action. It doesn't help to keep confessing the right things if you're continually thinking the wrong things. Working on your thought life is the only thing that will keep your thoughts from working on you. Either your thoughts have control of you through the power of the enemy or you have control of them through the power of God.

Every harmful thought that you do not bring into captivity will become a part of you. A thought pattern can become a way of life. If you accept any thought that is contrary to God's word you will have allowed a stronghold to be built in your mind that eventually will have to be pulled down. II Corinthians 10:4-5 says:

> *"for the weapons of our warfare are not of the flesh, but divinely powerful for the destruction of fortresses. We are destroying speculations and every lofty thing raised up against the knowledge of God, and we are taking every thought captive to the obedience of Christ,"*

We possess the mind of Christ but we still have the full capacity to think with the mind of the flesh. We are mentally bilingual. We think with the language we practice the most. Be careful to think in the right language.

The Emotions

Do you have any idea how many times God has been speaking to you but you were so upset, angry, stubborn, or consumed with negative emotions that you couldn't hear His voice? Your emotions are to your soul what your physical feelings are to your body. Emotions are God's indicators to let you know what is going on inside. If you live solely by your emotions, you risk failing to fulfill what God has purposed for your life and missing the blessings He has for you.

Your emotions can mislead you, so you have to anchor your soul with the Word of God in order to make it through the storms of life. Otherwise, it is possible to make one bad decision on a bad day that will negatively affect the rest of your life. If you find yourself frequently feeling angry or frustrated and you're not sure why or if you often feel depressed or experience a vague sense of unrest for no apparent reason, your soul is still in control. Learning not to allow feelings to dictate your behavior is extremely important. If you can learn to manage your feelings when they are out of line, sooner or later those feelings will come into line.

When you have an argument with someone, what do you usually do? Most people continue to replay in their minds the hurtful thing that was said. They may begin to believe what was said and want to get even. For example, if you believe a certain person doesn't like you, the enemy will put thoughts in your mind that will set you up to act in a way that may *cause* them not to like you. You must begin to react to such pain in a new way. You can pray, "Lord, help me to press through this feeling of rejection without speaking or acting in the wrong way."

Even though your emotions are fed by your physical senses, God is able to restore your deepest emotions that have been distorted over the course of your lifetime. He can guide you toward new ways of responding to people and situations. God wants to heal you from the inside out and to set you free from your harmful emotions.

We need to realize that worry, anxiety, and fear are sin. When you worry and fret, you are like a child who does not trust your parents to meet your needs. Jesus knew how to trust His Father. Remember the boat in the storm? The disciples were full of fear, believing they were all going to drown, but Jesus was in the back of the boat sleeping.

Why? His soul was free from the fear of dying, from the fear of sickness or anything else. He knew His purpose. He knew there was no way He was going to die in a storm at sea when His destiny was to die on a cross for you and me. Knowing that you, too, have a destiny gives you that same freedom from fear.

Responding to your emotions properly is an important step in keeping the devil from gaining a foothold in your life.

The Will

God created us with a free will. That ability "to think and to feel and then to choose" is what makes us different from all the rest of creation. When the other two areas of your soul are not renewed and restored your will will be misdirected. When your mind is constantly being bombarded or preoccupied with negative thinking or with false beliefs and you are consumed with painful emotions, your ability to choose what is right or what is God's will is seriously impaired. That's why it's never good to make important decisions during a crisis or when you're upset. These are the times your judgment is most likely coming from your soul rather than from your spirit. Don't see yourself or others through the natural eye. See yourself as God sees you. Confess: "I can do all things through Christ who strengthens me."

Here are some very helpful suggestions to guide you toward this goal:

1. Search the Scriptures for a word that speaks the mind of God to your specific situation.
2. Write these Scriptures on note cards.

3. Take these "truth cards" wherever you go and pull them out as necessary, speaking them out loud until the power of the negative thought or emotion is broken.
4. Be prepared to fight for your freedom with some radical choices.
5. Flood your mind with truth and with things that line up with the Word of God.

Following these steps will enable you to lose your will in God's will. Eventually you will desire what He desires, just as Psalm 37:4 promises: *"Delight yourself in the Lord; And He will give you the desires of your heart."*

The end result

So, what does it mean to control your flesh? It means allowing the Holy Spirit in you to dictate how you will react in any given situation. It means allowing your spirit, not your soul, to determine how you will respond to people and to circumstances.

The more you crucify your flesh, the more your spirit grows. Galatians 2:20 says, *"I have been crucified with Christ; and it is no longer I who live, but Christ lives in me; and the life which I now live in the flesh I live by faith in the Son of God, who loved me, and delivered Himself up for me."* It's so exciting to actually start being who you are in the Spirit. Believe it or not, you can consistently live strong in the Lord and in the power of His might. You can speak to your body or to your mind and call them into line.

Spiritual Surgery

You can begin to confess:

> I am not moved by my emotions.
> I will not accept depression, anger, or fear.
> I will have joy. The joy of the Lord is my strength.
> Frustrations will not dominate me.
> I have victory in Jesus' name.
> Regardless of the circumstances, regardless of what I see and hear,
> I am more than a conqueror.

It isn't easy. It takes determination and discipline, but you can do it. It's so much more satisfying to be powerful than pitiful, but you can't have it both ways.

Someone is looking to you for strength and hope. You must train yourself to exalt the Word of God above all reasoning, logic, and imaginations that are contrary to that Word. Luke 1:46-47 says, *"...My soul exalts the Lord, and my Spirit has rejoiced in God my Savior."* Hope is the anchor of the soul. Hebrews 6:18-19 says:

> *"in order that by two unchangeable things, in which it is impossible for God to lie, we may have strong encouragement, we who have fled for refuge in laying hold of the hope set before us. This hope we have as an anchor of the soul, a hope both sure and steadfast and one which enters within the veil,"*

When you become a son or a daughter who manifests the glory of God through your life, you have effectively dealt with your soul.

81

Chapter 8

Don't Drink the Poison

Don't Drink the Poison

In case you aren't familiar with the best way to poison someone, let me give you a quick lesson in "Elimination by Lethal Ingestion 101."

Name that poison

Most poisons are swallowed or inhaled into the body or injected directly into the blood stream. If you want to be really sneaky about it, you can poison someone over a long period of time until enough poison accumulates in their system that it finally takes over and begins to attack the nervous system or the stomach lining or the heart muscle -- whatever it's designed to destroy -- on its own.

I'm pretty sure that if someone offered you a free spoonful of arsenic, you wouldn't be in the least bit tempted to accept it. Yet the devil is using a sneaky, more subtle plan for poisoning your heart and your mind every day. He is continually administering small doses to you of the deadliest spiritual poison in existence: offense. The word "offense" comes from the Greek word *skandalon*. *Skandalon* is the name of the part of an animal trap that *holds the bait* to lure an animal into the trap. Offenses lure you into a trap. Once you are in the trap, you are --

TRAPPED! The Lord wants to open your eyes and make you aware of what's been happening so that you won't be tricked into drinking the spiritual poison any more.

Diagnosing its presence

Jesus warned us about the spiritual poison of the end times in Matthew 24:10-12:

> *"And at that time many will fall away and will deliver up one another and hate one another. And many false prophets will arise, and will mislead many. And because lawlessness is increased, most people's love will grow cold."*

Look at the progression this takes, beginning with a seemingly little thing like being offended.

1st You will distrust. This literally contaminates your mind so that your faith is weakened. Distrust leads you:
- to desert your post in the end-time army and to forsake praying for your brothers and sisters who are engaged in fierce spiritual battles, and
- to betray your brothers and sisters and fall into bitterness. How many times have you experienced this with someone close to you?
  - One or both of you became offended about something and you never really talk it through or reconcile.
  - Then you continue to see things about them that you don't like which are never discussed.

- Finally you begin to wonder how you could have ever been close to them in the first place.

2nd You will be open to <u>deception</u>. The fastest way to open yourself up to deception in every area of your life is to harbor bitterness or unforgiveness toward someone. When you choose to walk in offense, your disobedience blocks your ability to hear God.

3rd Your love will <u>grow cold</u>. You're even in danger of losing your heart for God and His people, because God is love.

Why does offense lead to distrust? Because offense takes over your heart and interferes with knowing and believing God. God is love. Resentment, anger, even a negative attitude, will all poison your spiritual life and affect your ability to believe God. Hebrews 11:6 tells us, *"And without faith it is impossible to please Him, for he who comes to God must believe that He is, and that He is a rewarder of those who seek Him."*

Why do you think that immediately after Jesus instructed the disciples in praying the prayer of faith, He said in Mark 11:24-25:

"Therefore I say to you, all things for which you pray and ask, believe that you have received them, and they shall be granted you. And whenever you stand praying, forgive, if you have anything against anyone; so that your Father also who is in heaven may forgive you your transgressions."

In essence He said, "Drop it. Let it go, so that you can be forgiven." Do you have any idea how many Christians are trying to believe God for things while they are full of offense? Then we even have enough nerve to blame God when our prayers go unanswered. Jesus plainly said that you can't have faith and be offended at the same time. You can't even have your sins forgiven if you don't forgive.

How often do you feel irritated or confused, like something's wrong but you're not quite sure what it is? How often have you been unable to hear God but you didn't understand why? Negative emotions could be edging out your faith, preventing you from fully believing that God loves you, wants to help you, and intends to be there for you.

Let's do a quick self-check here. After an argument or when someone really disappoints you, when someone says something to you or about you that really hurts, what do you usually do? Most of us replay it in our minds a few times. We think about it and then find someone to talk about it with. We may think about how we can get back at them or at least make them feel sorry or a little guilty for what they've said or done. We may even pray about it. Then when the Lord hears and answers, instead of leaving it there, we get up off our knees and go right back to thinking about it and talking about it, thinking about it and talking about it. This becomes an endless cycle. That's drinking the poison. Give it to God and leave it alone. Don't even touch that thing!

Being offended may not seem like such a terrible sin. If someone does something to hurt you, you have a right to be offended. Right? Wrong. Remember, the offense is the bait used to lure you into deeper, more deadly deceptions. The enemy's ultimate goal is for you to fall into confusion, manipulation, control, and worse. He will try to keep feeding you the poison in your thoughts a little at a time. The doses can be so small that you may have an attitude of offense without even being aware of it.

Remember, your flesh is not the least bit interested in living your life God's way. Your will is full of stubbornness and pride saying, "If I don't get my way, just forget it." Your mind is programmed with the influence of the world, so your thoughts insist, "I'm not going to apologize even if the Lord *is* dealing with me. I said I was sorry the last time, and anyway, I'm not the one to blame. He should be apologizing to me." The only problem is that no one ever wins the "blame game."

I used to think that the Christian thing to do when people would say or do things that hurt me or offended me was just to say nothing and to continue to be as nice to them as possible. I would pray for the grace to forgive them and for the pain to go away. In actuality, I was suppressing my true feelings, just pretending that everything was okay. I was tolerating the people as well as tolerating the pain because I truly believed that was my only choice. Eventually, this caused me to become physically ill. I was diagnosed with multiple sclerosis when I was in my early forties. I am now convinced that the manifestation of that disease in my body was partly a result of my years of suppressing tremendous emotional pain and not knowing what to do with my anger and disappointment. Praise the Lord, He healed me of MS along with everything else the enemy tried to put on me.

Even if you've given mental assent to refusing offense, the real test will come when you least expect it. How many times each day do you have an opportunity to be offended and you take the bait hook, line, and sinker? It isn't easy, but you can stop yourself and quit playing the enemy's blame game. You can't keep people from hurting you. Regardless of what other people say and do, God's way to respond is to say, "I'm not going to be resentful or even angry. I won't hang on to this or allow my mind to dwell on it." Just let it go.

The moment that painful thought comes to your mind, you have to tear it down and give it to the Lord. If you don't you're choosing to drink spiritual poison. II Corinthians 10:4-5 says:

> *"for the weapons of our warfare are not of the flesh, but divinely powerful for the destruction of fortresses. We are destroying speculations and every lofty thing raised up against the knowledge of God, and we are taking every thought captive to the obedience of Christ,"*

If you don't bring that thought into captivity, it will become a part of you. A thought pattern can become a way of life, leaving you with a victim mentality or with a complaining, angry, jealous, negative, critical spirit. You will wonder why you're never satisfied and why that bitter edge just won't go away. Eventually, you will have a stronghold that will have to be pulled down because you accepted that lie and drank the poison instead of drinking the water of life and the truth in the Word of God.

Once the poison is in your system, the enemy doesn't even have to hang around. The poison will spread through your mind and emotions and do even more damage on its own. You can be in the mall or in your car or on the phone and hear a certain song or see something that will trigger that pain and off you'll go into depression, anxiety, rejection, and any number of negative emotions. It doesn't really matter which one, because they all have the same effect, just as though you drank the poison again. God wants to end the poisonous thoughts that are still bringing pain and causing you unconsciously to inflict your pain upon those you love.

Love is the antidote

Now for the antidote. You know that if children get into the cleaning supplies or the medicine cabinet you can call the Poison Control Center for the antidote, something that will counteract the poison. God's antidote is love. John 13:34-35 says:

> *"A new commandment I give to you, that you love one another, even as I have loved you, that you also love one another. By this all men will know that you are My disciples, if you have love for one another."*

Love doesn't have hurt feelings over every little thing. Why? If you're walking in love, you're more concerned with what you can do for someone else than about what they have or haven't done for you. You're more concerned with why they did what they did or said what they said and how you can bring peace back into the relationship. You will be thinking "What's wrong in your life that you would do that to me? What's hurting inside you to make you act that way?" This may seem extreme, but when you are able to pray for people who are hurting you, you will be in control of the situation and God can use you because "love never fails."

Unforgiveness is a major source of many physical, emotional, psychological, and spiritual problems. You may think you have forgiven everyone who has hurt you in the past, but ask your body and your emotions if they agree with you. You're fooling yourself if you think you can do anything significant for God when you're irritated, agitated, frustrated, or acting any way other than walking in love.

If you're holding a grudge against someone right now, that grudge actually is holding you. The only way to guard against being deceived in this way and to protect yourself from opening your soul up to other forms of deception is to walk in love. We need to be quick to show mercy and quick to forgive. If you find yourself becoming angry, hurt, or upset, stop and realize "I'm in a bad place. I'm in danger of drinking spiritual poison," and repent. There will be times when people will say and do things that really do offend you and that really do hurt your feelings. It's still far better to say, "I refuse to be offended. I won't keep this pain. No poison for me, today. I'm giving this to You, Lord, right now. I forgive them, in Jesus' Name."

If you don't "shake it off" and you stay offended, resentment will soon follow and you'll find yourself sulking and stewing. Then you'll become bitter. There's no such thing as a "bitter, loving" Christian.

Remember, it's not the bite of the snake that kills you. It's the poison that's been injected into your blood stream. You may have received an emotional blow a long time ago when your dad left or when your husband walked out on you. Then you took another one when your best friend betrayed you or when you lost your job. You may be struggling to understand why your child died when you prayed and prayed and begged God to intervene. The wounds from these traumas may have closed up, but the poison is still there.

Proverbs 17:9 says, *"He who covers a transgression seeks love, But he who repeats a matter separates intimate friends."* The Amplified version reads, *"He who covers and forgives an offense seeks love, but he who repeats or harps on a matter separates even close friends."* If you really love someone, you *do* overlook their mistakes, give them the benefit of the doubt, and always believe the best of them. It's not easy to humble yourself, to go to someone and say you're sorry even when you don't really believe you've done anything wrong. It's not easy to let something go that you'd really like to make a major issue of, especially if you could easily win your case in any court of law. I John 4:16-21 says:

> *"And we have come to know and have believed the love which God has for us. God is love, and the one who abides in love abides in God, and God abides in him. By this, love is perfected with us, that we may have confidence in the day of judgment; because as He is, so also are we in this world. There is no fear in love; but perfect love casts out fear, because fear involves punishment, and the one who fears is not perfected in love. We love, because He first loved us. If someone says, 'I love God,' and hates his brother, he is a liar; for the one who does not love his brother whom he has seen, cannot love God whom he has not seen. And this commandment*

we have from Him, that the one who loves God should love his brother also."

Forgiveness is the treatment

Forgiveness is a choice. You control the process. No one can force you to forgive, and the person being forgiven doesn't have to participate or even cooperate. Since God commands you to forgive, it is something He will help you to do.

Have you ever asked the question, "How can I possibly forgive what he or she did to me?" The answer is: "You can't." You alone do not have the ability to forgive. You will only be able to forgive out of a heart that is filled with the love of God.

Forgiving doesn't free the person who hurt you from the consequences of their behavior. It sets *you* free from the torment of unforgiveness and the bitterness that eats away on the inside of you. If you don't let offenders off your hook, you will remain hooked to them and to your past. To stop the pain, you have to let them go. Your being upset with someone and refusing to forgive them has the same affect on you spiritually as if *you* were to drink poison and stand there expecting *them* to drop dead.

Relationships that last and grow strong do so not because you never hurt each other, not because you never have an opportunity to be offended, not even because you were able to forget what they did that hurt you, but because you value the relationship so you choose to forgive.

Don't Drink the Poison

Your need to forgive isn't an issue between you and the person who hurt you. It's between you and God. Forgiveness is agreeing to live with the consequences of another person's sin. That's what Jesus did for you. You must believe God for the grace to forgive every person who ever left you, disappointed you, or offended you in any way. Otherwise you'll keep taking it out on other people or on yourself. The length of the forgiveness process is usually proportionate to the severity of the pain and to your determination to let it go. When the offense is severe, the process of forgiveness can be equally severe.

If you're the one who is receiving forgiveness, be patient, and help your spouse or your friend through the hard times. You must also forgive yourself for your mistakes and poor choices. You must believe that the Blood of Jesus has enough power to cleanse every stain and to remove every pain. Our Lord made a way for you to miss the mess and avoid a life consisting of living through one emotional crisis after another. People who don't know Jesus don't have that same freedom.

There are numerous examples in God's hall of fame of men and women who were used mightily by God because they turned away from offense and stayed the course to their destinies.

> David ignored his brothers' insults and went on to tackle Goliath.

> Noah was the butt of everyone's jokes, but he just kept hammering.

Joseph was severely mistreated, but his faith and refusal to fall into self-pity took him from the pit to the palace.

Paul in II Timothy 4:16 said, *"At my first defense no one supported me, but all deserted me; may it not be counted against them."* Putting his own needs aside, he had put his life on the line to bring the gospel to these people. Then at the first sign of trouble, every last one of them deserted him. He could have been offended, but he refused to drink the devil's poison. Instead of throwing himself a pity party, he prayed: "May it not be charged against them."

Jesus' truth and righteousness caused offense to the citizens of Nazareth when He tried to minister in his hometown. They said, "Who does He think He is? He's only a carpenter's son!" Don't be surprised when it offends people to see God using you and not them. Never forget that God will use whom He wants, when He wants, where He wants, and a person who *will* is the person God can use.

Steps in the process of true forgiveness:

1. Acknowledge your hurt and anger.
2. Realize that holding onto the pain only hinders *you.*
3. Consciously let go of any need for revenge.
4. Pray for the one who hurt you, asking God to heal the wounds that caused them to harm you.
5. Pray that your wounds don't cause you to bring pain upon those you love.

Prayer:

Lord, I choose to exercise the authority You have given me through the Name of Jesus to speak to my soul.
I break the bondage of rejection, anger, unforgiveness, and bitterness from myself.
Just as Psalm 19:14 says, "Let the words of my mouth and the meditation of my heart be acceptable in Your sight, O Lord, my rock and my Redeemer."
In Jesus' Name.

Chapter 9

Faith Fatalities

E ven in your newfound freedom the enemy will be stirring up troubles designed to tear down everything you've been taught to believe about your God. Satan is continually planning strategies to undermine your faith. You will be walking through some things you haven't anticipated. You will encounter some unexpected twists and turns. I call these strategies "Faith Fatalities."

This is the season when "everything that can be shaken is being shaken." The enemy will try to take advantage of anything you're going through to cause you to suffer a Faith Fatality. The Lord will use this as an opportunity for your faith to grow to another level. God is looking for a people who will quote Romans 8:31: *"What then shall we say to these things? If God is for us, who is against us?"* He is looking for sons and daughters who will say, "I don't understand what I'm going through right now. I can't explain it, but if God is for me, it doesn't matter who's against me. My faith is in Him."

Faith is trusting and believing.
>Faith can't be intellectualized.
>>Nothing in the Kingdom of God succeeds
>>without faith.

Hebrews 11:6a says, *"And without faith it is impossible to please Him."* Simply saying you have faith is not enough. Your true level of faith will be reflected in your actions. True faith will cause you to see the invisible, hear the inaudible, touch the intangible, believe the impossible, and "speak those things which are not as though they are."

Hebrews 11:6b says, *"for he who comes to God must believe that He is, and that He is a rewarder of those who seek Him."* As your faith grows, when you hear a word from the Lord or find a promise in the Bible pertaining to your situation, you will be able to say with confidence, "This is what my God says about it, and I trust in Him. Nothing is going to move me or steal my faith."

Still, as God's demands stretch your faith, you will experience times when you stumble and struggle. The contrast between your vision of what one day will be and the reality of your repeated ups and downs can definitely tend to dampen your enthusiasm. The most distressing thing to a Christian, especially once you know God's call on your life and you're trying to walk in it, is that sense of despair and unrest that creeps into your thoughts and interrupts your sleep when the vision you've seen and the reality you're living in are far apart. This is what I call "a situation that isn't lining up with your revelation."

One of my own Faith Fatalities was that each time I heard a word from the Lord, I would run off to make it happen in my own strength, rather than doing what God wanted done in the right way, in the right time, and in the right place. As a result, I wasted considerable time and energy on works of the flesh and experienced untold frustration over the lack of results.

Think about the birthing table in a hospital. It is actually designed to keep an expectant mother in position in spite of the pain of labor and delivery. That is what your love for God and the vision He has given you is meant to do. It holds you in place even when you would like to step out of the will of God to save yourself the stress and discomfort of the process. Jesus tied Himself to the birthing table in the garden of Gethsemane. The Church and our salvation was in Him "from the foundation of the world" and it was to be brought out of Him on the Cross. As the pains became greater, He prayed to change position. He begged in Luke 22:42: *"Father, if You be willing, remove this cup from Me. Nevertheless not My will, but Thine, be done."*

Your Heavenly Father is asking you, "Will you maintain your position, even when it means that you will be exposed to a high level of pain?"

Faith Fatality #1: THE WAIT

One of the most effective strategies the enemy uses against you is "the wait." God's Word repeatedly exhorts us to "hold fast." Hebrews 3:6 says, *"but Christ was faithful as a Son over His house whose house we are, if we hold fast our confidence and the boast of our hope firm until the end."*

It's easy to hold on for ten minutes, or even ten hours. Some can even hang on for ten days or two weeks. The challenge comes when it's been ten months or ten years and you're still waiting to see the word that God has spoken in your spirit come to pass in the natural realm. What do you do then?

What if nothing -- absolutely nothing -- is happening and God is silent? What if it seems that He's turning a deaf ear to your prayers?

Abraham and Sarah had a *long* wait for Isaac.

Moses spent forty years on the backside of the mountain before he was sent forth with the authority to set his people free.

David waited seventeen years from the time he was anointed king to when he was actually sitting on the throne.

Mary and Martha didn't understand why Jesus didn't come when they first called for Him.

Paul waited until he reached heaven to be free of his "thorn in the flesh."

Waiting tests our faith. As a loving Father and a Master Teacher, God knows we must pass the tests on our own. So remember, when the Teacher is not talking, He is testing. When God is silent, He expects you to put what you've already been taught to work in your situation.

There are two primary challenges during "the wait." First, you must learn to ignore every voice that does not line up with the Word of God. Have you ever noticed that when

God is *silent*, every other voice seems so *loud*? That inner voice of doubt: "You never heard God anyhow." That inner voice of fear: "You're going to lose everything." The nagging memories from your past: "Do you really think God could forgive *that*?" These are only lies designed to undermine your faith.

The other challenge is the insecurity of never knowing exactly how long a test will last. However, the Word repeatedly assures you that standing fast against this Faith Fatality will be worth "the wait." Psalm 27:13-14 says:

> *"I would have despaired unless I had believed that I would see the goodness of the Lord In the land of the living. Wait for the Lord; Be strong, and let your heart take courage; Yes, wait for the Lord."*

You may have waited and waited, wondering if the answer will *ever* come. I've heard it said that God will seemingly take forever to do something suddenly. When your suddenly comes, I promise it will have been well worth "the wait."

Hold fast because your God is faithful!
Faith is hanging on to *nothing*
Until that nothing becomes *everything*
You're believing God for in your life.

Hebrews 11:1 (KJV): *"Now faith is the substance of things hoped for, the evidence of things not seen."*

Faith Fatality #2: THE STORM

What do you do when it seems like all hell is breaking loose around you and you can't seem to find God anywhere?

Storms come in many forms, but they are always a strategy of the enemy designed to blow you as far off course as possible. They may be storms he provokes *you* into stirring up or they may be storms you get drawn into after he has provoked someone else.

Storms may come frequently or infrequently in your life. They may last a few days or a few weeks. They may come during times when you are busy pursuing God's plan for your life or they may come during long waits for your prayers to be answered. Storms test our faith just as waits do. The difference is that a storm is generally more chaotic and of shorter duration than a wait.

Sometimes our own issues bring on the storm:

> Abraham's and Sarah's impatience and eagerness to help God fulfill His promise resulted in the birth of a son to Sarah's handmaiden. This "work of the flesh" brought chaos and confusion, not to mention jealousy, heartbreak, and emotional pain to everyone involved. We are still suffering from the strife between the nations that are descended from those two sons.
>
> Moses had an anger issue that resulted in his killing an Egyptian, forcing him to flee for his own life. After a forty-year wait, God called him to lead the

Israelites out of Egypt. These rebellious people brought storm after storm against him. Unfortunately for Moses, he fell back into anger and "struck the rock" rather than speaking to it as God had instructed, costing him his entry into the Promised Land.

Jacob's trickery and manipulation brought the storms of a hasty escape, an unhappy marriage, and a huge family feud. Many years later he was still uncertain of his brother's feelings and feared for his life while returning home as God had instructed him to do.

David's disobedience even after becoming king led to storms of violence, betrayal, and lust which never left his house.

Remember in Mark 4 when Jesus was teaching the multitudes by the seaside? He spent the entire day using parables to paint pictures about faith and believing the Word of the Lord. Then in verse 35 it says, *"On that day... He said to them, 'Let us go over to the other side.'"* The disciples sent the multitude away and boarded the boat. They hadn't gone far when a great storm arose. You know the story: they panicked, afraid that they were all going to drown. They cried out for Jesus to wake up, but He was asleep on a pillow in the back of the boat. When they finally woke Jesus, they were asking, "Teacher, do you not care that we are perishing?" Jesus replied to the disciples, saying in effect, "Didn't you get anything out of the parables? Do you still have so little faith? I spent all day teaching you and you flunked the test on the material." *He wanted them to hold on to His word while they waited out the storm. He had spoken that they were going to the other side, and that's what He intended, storm or no storm.*

Have you ever done the same thing the disciples did that day? Have you ever gotten a word that really encouraged you and lifted your spirit only to be hit by a storm? Have you ever gotten some news that rocked your boat and made you feel overwhelmed, like you were about to go under, just as the disciples did when Jesus was sleeping in the back of the boat? It's a typical human reaction to panic and to cry out in your fear:

> Jesus, how can you be so calm when I'm so confused? God, do you care? Are you there? Lord, do You have any idea how hard it is to pray under all this stress? To work under all this pressure? To smile when I can barely hold back the tears?

Storms test our faith. Again, as a loving Father and a Master Teacher, God knows we must pass the test on our own. So remember, when the Teacher is not talking, He is testing. When God is silent, He expects you to put what you've already been taught to work in your situation.

God has given you everything you need to go through any storm you're in all the way to "the other side." You can't be like the disciples in the boat. You must remember in the storm what you were taught in the sunshine. You know from I John 5:14-15: *"This is the confidence that we have in Him, that, if we ask anything according to His will, He hears us. And if we know that He hears us, whatsoever we ask, we know that we have the things that we asked Him for."* And Psalm 34:17 promises, *"When the righteous cry,*

the Lord hears, and delivers them out of all their troubles."
Not some, but *all*.

The test is that you never know exactly how long it will be
from the time you cry out to God until you see the answer
manifested in your situation. One of my favorite scriptures
is Philippians 4:6-7:

> *"Don't worry about anything. But in everything by*
> *prayer and supplication with thanksgiving, let your*
> *requests be made known unto God. And the peace*
> *of God, which passes all understanding, will keep*
> *your hearts and minds through Christ Jesus."*

I know it's true that the peace of God which is beyond my
comprehension will keep my heart and my mind not simply
because I've read it a few times. I know it's true because at
one point I endured a storm in my soul that almost caused
me to lose my mind. I know it's true because I've spent
many sleepless nights struggling with problems that
seemed overwhelming and fearing that my situation was
hopeless. I entertained the enemy's lies that I would never
"get it together" again and that I had far too many faults
and character flaws for the Lord to use me. I'd cry, "Lord,
you said your peace would keep my heart and my mind, but
I'm in torment. What am I missing?" Finally the Spirit of
the Lord brought a revelation to my spirit that it's not
enough to have a word or even to know a word. You've got
to believe it and stand on it and make it work for you.

I've learned that God will allow you to be tested in the
areas in which you are weak in order to make you strong.
The Holy Spirit wants to show you that His Word works in
your situation so that you will not be overwhelmed in that

area again. When the heat is on, He'll show up in the fire with you if you simply stand on His Word.

Faith Fatality #3: FEAR

Fear is the opposite of faith. Fear disregards the awesome power of God.

Fear is as lethal as paralysis of the brain. Fear affects your thoughts and makes your memory sluggish. Fear is often irrational, but no less real. Fear may express itself in anger. Fear eventually becomes impossible to hide. Fear is not prejudiced. Fear attacks everyone.

Fear operates by the same laws as faith. If faith causes good things to happen, fear -- as a Faith Fatality -- will do the same thing in reverse. Fear is a connector just as faith is a connector. The fear of death can connect you to the illness you fear. The fear of lack can connect you to the unemployment line. The fear of people can bring disapproval and anxiety.

Fear is not okay! You must not tolerate fear. Fear that is tolerated will be faith that is contaminated. Fear grants Satan access into your life just as the shield of faith will keep him out. Take away fear and you close the door to this particular Faith Fatality.

Acting on your fear may cause the very thing you fear to come to pass in your life. Just ask Job. The following excerpts from Job's story show us that he paid a high price for his fear:

Job 1:4-5: *"And his sons used to go and hold a feast in the house of each one on his day, and they would send and invite their three sisters to eat and drink with them. And it came about, when the days of feasting had completed their cycle, that Job would send and consecrate them, rising up early in the morning and offering burnt offerings according to the number of them all; for Job said, 'Perhaps my sons have sinned and cursed God in their hearts.' Thus Job did continually."*

Job 1:13, 18-19: *"Now it happened on the day when his sons and his daughters were eating and drinking wine in their oldest brother's house, ... While he was still speaking, another also came and said, 'Your sons and your daughters were eating and drinking wine in their oldest brother's house, and behold, a great wind came from across the wilderness and struck the four corners of the house, and it fell on the young people and they died; and I alone have escaped to tell you.'"*

Job 3:25: *"For what I fear comes upon me, And what I dread befalls me."*

We know that faith without works is dead. Fear without a corresponding action will also die. You can defeat your fears by not allowing them to influence your behavior or your speech.

The Bible speaks of two kinds of fear: the kind we know as "being afraid" and the kind we know as "reverential fear." The contrast between "being afraid" and reverence is as real as the contrast between condemnation and conviction.

111

A loving Father doesn't want His children to be afraid of Him. He wants us to reverence Him. He may not always agree with what you've done, but He always loves *who* you are.

You have to be honest about your fears, face them, and ask the Lord to reveal the lies you have believed and to set you free from them.

Are you troubled by any of these fears?

- Fear of Failure causes you to avoid or delay doing something for fear of not doing it well enough. This fear will rob you of your vision and cause you to accept compromise. No one should consciously instill life-limiting thoughts into others, but sometimes people do. Others may stop you or slow you down temporarily, but you are the only one who can do it permanently.
- Fear of Rejection causes you to avoid or delay doing something because you are consistently more concerned with what other people think than with what pleases God. Family members and even religious folk can be cruel, spiteful, and selfish, creating this kind of fear and immobility.
- Fear of not being needed is a fear that affects people who have a "need to be needed." This fear causes a mother or caregiver to adopt co-dependent behaviors such as manipulation and "false guilt" to perpetuate being needed by someone else. This fear sometimes becomes apparent when the caregiver experiences the "empty nest syndrome" or something similar.

- <u>Fear of not being in control</u> is when you are afraid of everything falling apart if you are not "in charge." It can be shame-, fear-, or anger-based. It can cause you to be manipulative and may even express itself in violent behavior.
- <u>Fear of loneliness</u> is often seen in conjunction with rejection and insecurity. This fear can cause you to choose unwholesome friends out of desperation, or to drive away the very people that you care about. God wants you to be so secure in your relationship with Him that you can be alone but never feel lonely again.
- <u>Fear of authority figures</u> causes you to find it extremely difficult to submit in marriage, on the job, or in church. This fear distorts reality and will cause you to distrust employers, pastors, or anyone in leadership positions. This fear becomes evident when you have problems with receiving correction.

Acknowledgment of fear is the first step to victory. Believing 2 Timothy 1:7 is the next step: (KJS) *"For God hath not given us the spirit of fear; but of power, and of love, and of a sound mind."* As you gain victory over each fear, you will begin to feel less threatened. You will be able to accept change more readily. You will experience more joy. You will be able to walk in greater faith. You will begin to grow into the truth of 1 John 4:18: *"There is no fear in love; but perfect love casts out fear, because fear involves punishment, and the one who fears is not perfected in love."*

Faith Fatality #4: DISOBEDIENCE

One of the most difficult lessons for me to learn was that doing the will of God often means going against what I want to do. God calls us to a commitment of one hundred percent obedience. Deuteronomy 28:2 says,*"All these blessings will come on you and overtake you, if you will listen to the voice of the Lord."* This scripture essentially says: "If you want God's blessings, you must do what He says, no matter what."

James 2:14,21-22,26 explains how your faith is proved by your level of obedience to God:

> *"What use is it, my brethren, if a man says he has faith, but he has no works? Can that faith save him? ... Was not Abraham our father justified by works, when he offered up Isaac his son on the altar? You see that faith was working with his works, and as a result of the works, faith was perfected;... For just as the body without the spirit is dead, so also faith without works is dead."*

The enemy uses your disobedience as a Faith Fatality. He knows that if you're a child of God who hasn't learned to hear *and obey* the voice of your Father, he can still bring deception and chaos into your life. What's wrong with this picture: you keep praying for God to bring change, bring breakthrough, bring freedom from anxiety, but...

> you keep doing the same things you've always done,

you keep thinking the same way you've always thought, and

you keep talking the same way you've always talked?

If you want change, breakthrough, and freedom, doesn't it make sense that you are going to have to do some things differently?

You might even be doing all the right things in many areas, but avoiding the *one* thing God has told you to do that *you* just don't want to do. You need to stop being more concerned about pleasing yourself than you are about pleasing God. I Samuel 15:22-23 says:

> *"And Samuel said, 'Has the Lord as much delight in burnt offerings and sacrifices As in obeying the voice of the Lord? Behold, to obey is better than sacrifice, And to heed than the fat of rams. For rebellion is as the sin of divination, And insubordination is as iniquity and idolatry. Because you have rejected the word of the Lord, He has also rejected you from being king.'"*

Because Saul disobeyed the Word of the Lord, God rejected him as king. Continued disobedience to the leading of the Holy Spirit will put you in danger of forfeiting fulfillment of God's call on your life. If you're like I was, you may not even realize what you are doing because your behavior patterns, your habits, and the way you think and talk are so much a part of you. I believed I had a right to my own choices. I didn't. Acts 17:30 warns us: *"Therefore having overlooked the times of ignorance, God is now declaring to men that all everywhere should repent."*

The rules have changed. God is having to yank us out of our comfort zones because we haven't gone willingly. Disobedience that God has tolerated up to this time He is no longer allowing. People's hearts and attitudes and motives are being challenged. God is saying, "I love you too much to allow you to keep hurting yourself. I'm tired of you missing the blessings I have for you. There's too much at stake to keep doing business as usual."

We used to be able to suppress and hide our "issues," but the Spirit of the Lord is saying, "No more!" to lying, gossiping, jealousy, envy, religion, greed, selfishness, manipulation, homosexuality, idolatry, fornication, stubbornness, and pride. We can't blame all this on the devil, either. God gave us a will, and sometimes we simply *choose* to lie, *choose* to hate, *choose* not to forgive, *choose* to watch things we shouldn't watch and to listen to things we shouldn't listen to, *choose* to give in to selfishness and lust. That's called **disobedience.** Any of these "issues" that you're tolerating in your personality right now will eventually become a stronghold in your life that you *will* have to deal with. You will have to deal with them God's way. Don't be looking under the bed. Don't be looking inside the closet. Don't be looking at your parents or your mate or your kids. Look inside *you.* As Galatians 6:3-5 says:

> *"For if anyone thinks he is something when he is nothing, he deceives himself. But let each one examine his own work, and then he will have reason for boasting in regard to himself alone, and not in*

regard to another. For each one shall bear his own load."

Hebrews 5:8 says, *"Although He was a Son, He learned obedience from the things which He suffered."* You will never experience the fullness of God if you're not willing to go through hardships and trials like Jesus did to get it. Each of us must make a choice either to continue to make excuses for why we don't obey or simply to obey.

Ecclesiastes 10:8 warns: *"He who digs a pit may fall into it, and a serpent may bite him who breaks through a wall."* Like any good parent, God has established boundaries for our protection. When you cross those boundaries by willfully choosing to disobey -- doing what God has said **not** to do or refusing to do what He's told you to do -- you're out there on your own. You've broken through the hedge of protection, and the serpent may bite you.

The enemy will try to provoke you into misusing your God-given gifts and crossing the line into disobedience. It is dangerous to think you can do what seems right to you -- "right in your own eyes" -- and then ask God to tag along and bless you.

Prayer:

Lord, I want to be holy as You are holy.
Jesus, I am forever grateful that You, as the perfect, sinless, Lamb of God, made Your holiness available to me with your own Blood.
Holy Spirit, cover me with your cloak of humility.
Increase my faith.
I pray for a spirit of obedience in my life.

Lord, you said a broken and a contrite heart You will not despise.
I hide my unholiness in the wounds of Jesus Christ right now, as Moses hid himself in the cleft of the rock.
I ask You to forgive me, Lord, of any unconfessed thoughts, words, deeds, or motives in my heart that separate me from You.
With your help, Holy Spirit, I am committed to one-hundred percent obedience.
I choose to allow you to be Lord and King in my life.
In Jesus' Name.

Faith Fatality #5: DISCOURAGEMENT

Galatians 6:9 says, *"And let us not lose heart in doing good, for in due time we shall reap if we do not grow weary."*

Satan hopes that if he slows you down you will wear out before you fulfill your God-given vision. That's why he attacks your faith so hard with this Faith Fatality.

I recently heard a story about the devil having a garage sale. There was a sign on the table which read "My Most Effective Tools Against Christians." Each tool on the table had a price tag on it. There were things like envy, jealousy, strife, grumbling and complaining, backbiting, distractions, and unforgiveness. One of the shoppers asked why the tool that seemed the most worn and soiled had the highest price tag on it when some of the others were obviously in better condition. "Why does this cost so much when some of the other things look almost brand new?" The enemy replied, "Because even when all of these other tools fail, this one works every time. It stops them in their tracks. It causes them to turn around, maybe even give up. This tool will keep some folks from ever fulfilling their destiny. DISCOURAGEMENT: this is the one I use most. It leads to despondency, despair, hopelessness, and ultimately, people will feel they have no reason even to go on living."

The enemy of your soul will literally orchestrate circumstances and bring situations into your life to discourage you. You get your hopes up. You get all excited. You dare to dream again and look forward to something really significant happening for you. Then comes the discouragement, the punch in the gut that knocks the wind out of you, that makes you feel sad and confused and tired and afraid to even keep trying. That's exactly the reaction the enemy was working for. He tries to get your eyes off your awesome God and onto the people or the circumstances. We've been forewarned in John 10:10 that he's out to kill, steal, and destroy everything God has for us: *"The thief comes only to steal and kill and destroy; I came that they might have life, and might have it abundantly."*

The first step in avoiding this Faith Fatality is not to place your expectations on people. People *will* disappoint you. No pastor is perfect. No parent has all the answers. No man can meet all of a woman's needs and no woman can meet all of a man's needs. God made us with a vacant space in our innermost being that only *He* can fill. He alone will never change or disappoint you. Malachi 3:6a says, *"For I, the Lord, do not change."* Our God is the same yesterday, today, and forever. God knows that disappointment leads to discouragement. He will allow you to experience disappointment with people again and again until you realize that you must continually encourage yourself in

Him. This means "to remind yourself of His goodness and faithfulness to you."

Feeling discouragement is not a sin, but how you handle that emotion when it comes is crucial. The devil will prod you to open your mouth and say things you shouldn't say. But Philippians 2:14 warns us: *"Do all things without grumbling and faultfinding and complaining against God and questioning and doubting among yourselves."* In other words, whatever you do, stop complaining and only use your mouth to praise God for His abundant grace. 1Thessalonians 5:18 says, *"in everything give thanks; for this is God's will for you in Christ Jesus."* Notice, it doesn't say *for* everything, but *in* everything. No matter how discouraging or how serious the conditions you are facing, the most important thing is to remember that "breakthrough comes from breaking through, continuing to press through no matter what."

If your happiness depends upon the faithfulness of people or upon favorable circumstances you are really in trouble because people and circumstances are always changing and not everything in life will go your way. Standing strong against discouragement will take both the grace of God and your determination not to be a Faith Fatality.

Prayer

Lord, I praise You, even in this ugly situation.
I thank You for the grace to make it through because I trust You and I know that You love me.
I believe, beyond a shadow of a doubt, that You will somehow work this all out for my good.
In Jesus' Name.

Chapter 10

Personal Prisons

A stronghold – or "personal prison" -- is any thought pattern or behavior contrary to the will of God that has essentially become a part of you. It's hard for God's blessings to catch up with you when you have become locked in a prison of negative thoughts and emotions.

Satan's strategy is to introduce his thoughts and ideas into your mind and to deceive you into believing that they are yours.

> It happened to King David. I Chronicles 21:1 tells us, *"Then Satan stood up against Israel and moved David to number Israel."* This was an act God had forbidden, but David acted on Satan's idea. David was a godly man and he wouldn't have knowingly obeyed the evil one. But what if the idea just "slipped" into his mind?

> I doubt that Judas realized where the idea to betray Jesus originated. But John 13:2 tells us, *"And during supper, the devil having already put into the*

heart of Judas Iscariot, the son of Simon, to betray Him."

Ananias and Sapphira might have thought that it was their own idea to withhold some of their offering while gaining the admiration and attention from the other Christians who believed they had given everything. Where did the idea really come from?

When I think of personal prisons, I picture things that still trouble us from childhood such as traumas or victimizations or things seemingly as harmless as rationalizations. We use these to keep bad habits and destructive thought patterns in our mental closet. It's no longer a secret that in our society many intelligent, well-educated people from all economic backgrounds still struggle with sexual sins, fear of men or fear of women, an inability to love, or an inability to trust. Even Christians suffer from compulsions to steal, to overeat, to gossip and complain, or to lie. Others have a root of bitterness or are victims of depression, doubt, and loneliness. Far too many believers are simply never able to be satisfied, always wanting more.

When the pressure is on, when you get really "hot," when a situation reaches a certain temperature, your temper kicks in. Your stubbornness, your bitterness, or your anger rears up. That's how the enemy works on you. The corruption is already engrafted into your mind, your will, and your emotions. You will almost automatically fall into behaviors that will bring the things you dread upon yourself.

When you begin to agree with negative opinions that other people have of you, when you buy into lies that you are a product of your past or that you are defined by your present condition, the enemy doesn't have to continue the attack. You will self-destruct from the inside. These thought patterns will cause you to be defeated not by what others think of you but by what you think of yourself.

God wants to break the automatic curses in the self-made prison of your heart. He wants you to begin to focus on what He's done *for* you instead of what's been done *to* you. God wants to take you to another level of deliverance where you won't have to keep going to an altar or into your prayer closet for the same thing week after week. Remember, *"whom the Son sets free is free indeed."*

For every time you've been hurt or wounded, God has an appointed time to heal you, and I believe this is your time. Your Heavenly Father is tired of so many of His kids being depressed and on all kinds of medication, taking pills to go to sleep and pills to get up. He is saying, "Child, you don't have to live like this." You must be determined to find that place in God where the devil can't put his finger on you so easily.

Self-will -- believing that we know more about what's best for us than God does -- is the source of many strongholds. Having a legitimate need but seeking to meet it in our own way rather than God's way can open the door to a stronghold. A stronghold does not have to be a demon. It can simply be the result of an unsubmitted self-will.

Once you allow your mind to dwell on a thought planted by the enemy, it automatically triggers an emotion. You will eventually act based on that emotion and "own" the behavior. You are responsible for the results at this stage because you failed to take that thought captive when it first appeared at the threshold of your mind. If you continue to repeat that behavior pattern for an extended period of time you will have formed a habit. If you exercise that habit long enough, a stronghold will become established. Once a stronghold of thought-and-response is entrenched in your mind, you almost lose your ability to choose to act contrary to that pattern of behavior. Those patterns of thinking and responding have formed strongholds in your mind. We can always find an excuse for not surrendering areas of our lives to the authority of Christ, but we will end up in another bondage. Never forget that bondage exists where a stronghold persists.

We all have "issues." If you were raised in a home where there was any form of interference in God's plan for your family, you will probably have at least one of these symptoms of a stronghold in your life:

1. An unhealthy sense of normal *(in some homes, fighting is normal)*
2. A need for control *(sometimes disguised as setting high standards)*
3. Rigid expectations *(and withdrawal of approval when not met)*
4. Fear of failure *(often disguised as habitual procrastination)*
5. A distorted sense of truth *(I'm okay. We're all okay.)*
6. Low self esteem *(may appear as a lack of motivation)*
7. Finding excuses *(blaming anyone but yourself for what's wrong)*

8. Overly sensitive or easily offended *(The supersensitive person has usually been hurt deeply and has scars on the inside from constantly reaching out for love and approval but receiving just the opposite. You see things other people don't see and tend to feel things other people don't feel because you read your hurt into each situation.)*

9. Self-righteousness and pride *(so spiritual acting you make people uncomfortable)*

10. Craving approval *(will do almost anything for praise or attention)*

11. Shallow relationships *(an emotionally deprived person tends to bond with another person on a similar level of emotional pain)*

12. Uncomfortable in social settings *(often feeling anxious and awkward, unwanted and insecure)*

13. Impulsive behavior *(Seeming to go from one crisis to another while never understanding why you have such a traumatic life; tending to "move" without seeing the alternatives or possible consequences of certain behaviors)*

14. Unrealistic sense of your ability *(This happens when parents were inconsistent. Certain behaviors were sometimes acceptable but at other times they brought anger or punishment. You had no honest way of evaluating yourself or your abilities. Demanding parents either failed to value your talents and abilities or caused you to believe you could never be good enough no matter how hard you tried)*

15. Legalistic *(attempting to please God and others by following a set of rules)*

16. Sense of unworthiness *(too often plagued with a continuous feeling of anxiety, inadequacy, and*

inferiority, and an inner nagging that says, "I'm not good. I'll never amount to anything. No one could ever possibly love me. Everything I do is wrong.")

17. Perfectionist Compulsion (*that inner feeling that says, "I never do anything quite well enough. I can't please myself, others, or God, no matter how hard I try." Always groping, striving, usually feeling guilty, driven by inner "oughts and shoulds," ever striving but never quite reaching the goal*)

18. Selfishness (*beyond normal with a cold, uncaring, insensitive attitude toward God, the church, and other people, The enemy has you all wrapped up in trying to take care of yourself, always ·praying: "What about me? Who's going to meet my needs?"*)

After looking through the list above, ask yourself these questions:

Do I see any familiar thought patterns, habits, or behaviors that lead me away from God's will for my life?

Do I struggle with negative thoughts and emotions about myself or my identity?

Do I struggle with believing and receiving God's unconditional love for me?

Do I experience uncontrolled feelings of jealousy, fear, anger, or lust on a regular basis?

Remember, a stronghold can be anything from compulsive eating to paranoia, from bitterness to obsessive love. Hostility is a stronghold. Inferiority is a stronghold.

Confusion is a stronghold. Manipulation is a stronghold. Homosexuality is a stronghold. Anorexia and bulimia are strongholds. Any negative thoughts and actions you cannot control spring from a stronghold. Somewhere in the past you consciously or unconsciously formed a pattern of thinking and behaving which now controls you. Don't think that simply putting on the armor of God at this stage will solve your dilemma. These strongholds are already entrenched and fortified.

All strongholds have several things in common:

1. Every stronghold is related to something we have exalted to a higher position than God in our lives.
2. Every stronghold pretends to bring something we feel we must have: help, comfort, stress relief, protection, etc.
3. Every stronghold in the life of a believer is a tremendous source of pride for the enemy, so he fuels your mind with deception to keep it standing.
4. At some point we realize we no longer control our strongholds, they control us.

These strongholds are like concrete fortresses we've constructed block by block over the course of our lifetime as protective mechanisms and survival skills. Each of these strongholds can be broken if you admit their existence and ask the Lord to reveal the truth about how each of them was established and to help you to tear them down.

Prison Cell #1: IDOLATRY

God has commanded, *"Thou shalt have no other Gods before Me,"* but we do, all of the time, without even realizing it. Idolatry is putting other people or things before God. Leviticus 26:1,14-16, and 30:

> *"'You shall not make for yourselves idols, nor shall you set up for yourselves an image or a sacred pillar, nor shall you place a figured stone in your land to bow down to it; for I am the Lord your God... 'But if you do not obey Me and do not carry out all these commandments, if, instead, you reject My statutes, and if your soul abhors My ordinances so as not to carry out all My commandments, and so break My covenant, I, in turn, will do this to you: I will appoint over you a sudden terror, consumption and fever that shall waste away the eyes and cause the soul to pine away; also, you shall sow your seed uselessly, for your enemies shall eat it up....I then will destroy your high places, and cut down your incense altars, and heap your remains on the remains of your idols; for My soul shall abhor you.'"*

God expects us to put Him first in our lives by loving Him *most*. This is evidenced by how much of our time, our thoughts, our motives, and our desires are centered around Him. Anything that we honor or exalt above Him in our thoughts or imaginations becomes an idol. James 4:4 says, *"You adulteresses, do you not know that friendship with the world is hostility toward God? Therefore whoever wishes to be a friend of the world makes himself an enemy of God."*

A huge but rarely recognized stronghold which will definitely harm your relationship with the Lord is putting any person, family member, child, husband, wife, ministry partner, or business associate ahead of the Lord in your time, your thoughts, your motives, or your desires. We readily recognize adultery, theft, or murder as sin, but we can be blind to the fact that anything we allow to grow up between us and our relationship with God is idolatry. Idolatry is not only an abomination to God, but an open invitation for spiritual disaster.

To find true peace and to have a satisfying relationship with your Lord you have to recognize and eliminate any type of idolatry. People have been worshipping some of these idols for years, and only the power of God can topple them.

> Many people find their fulfillment in their careers and allow their jobs to consume their thoughts and spare time.

> Others idolize their children. Nothing could be more reflective of the heart of God than a mother's love for her child. Yet, if that love passes the bounds of healthy affection into overprotection and obsession you will have a stronghold. Dragging kids to ballet, ball games, PTA, and music lessons, and making them do all the things you always wanted to do, either to fulfill your dreams or to fill the void in your life, is damaging to both of you.

> Sometimes even food or shopping can become an idol. If you often find yourself overeating or constantly shopping you could be attempting to use these activities to fill a void that only God can fill.

> Prolonged desperation, like that experienced by a couple who has been waiting for a child or a single

adult who has been longing to be married, often opens the door to the prison of idolatry. After their prayers are finally answered, they sometimes begin to idolize the gift rather than the Giver.

This may sound extreme, but stop and consider what you use to fill the empty places in your life. You were created with a holy hunger that only God can fill. This void will demand attention. We look desperately for something to satisfy us and to fill the empty place. Our craving to be filled is so strong that the moment something or someone seems to meet our need, we feel an overwhelming temptation to worship it. Isaiah 44:20 says, *"He feeds on ashes; a deceived heart has turned him aside. And he cannot deliver himself, nor say, 'Is there not a lie in my right hand?'"*

You don't have to love something or someone to idolize or exalt them in your mind. You can just as easily make an idol of something you hate if you allow it to steal your focus away from the Lord. Obsession that flows from putting someone in the place of God is sin. God is not the one who gives others the power to affect your destiny. Don't you give that power to others, either.

Grief is not sin. Nothing could be more natural than grieving the loss of a loved one. But if years later you're still completely consumed with the loss and your bitterness is blocking your relationship with your Heavenly Father, you have a problem. Refusing to allow God to minister comfort and healing to you over the passage of much time reveals a level of grief that has become a stronghold.

If you are holding on to anything or if there is something you are craving other than God for satisfaction right now, would you be willing to acknowledge it as a stronghold? How many times have we fed on ashes instead of feasting on the word of God or enjoying His sweet presence? I now pray daily that I will never again settle for anything less than God's best for me.

God is not condemning you. He is calling you to Himself.

Prison Cell #2: The Mighty Stronghold called REJECTION

Have you ever felt rejected? The dictionary definition for rejection is "refusing to grant a person recognition or acceptance, discarding that individual as being worthless or their feelings as unimportant to you." Everyone knows what it feels like to be criticized and rejected at times, even by the very people in our lives we desperately want to please. I believe God's definition for rejection is "a deception." The enemy begins as early in your life as possible by telling you lies like "No one truly loves you. You must be unworthy of love. You'll have to *do* something to get someone to love you. If you can't *do* what they want, you'll be rejected."

Life can be unfair. People can be hurtful.

> You may have felt rejected because your father was distant and cold, too busy to give you his time and attention. Or maybe he left and you're not sure why, or he wasn't ever there at all.

You may have felt rejected if your mother favored your sister who was prettier or your brother who was smarter than you.

You may have felt rejected because you weren't gifted with athletic ability and when the class divided up on teams you were always the last one chosen.

You may have experienced rejection in high school when you weren't invited to parties or the prom.

You may have felt the sting of rejection when you were passed over for a promotion at work.

You may have been in a relationship for a long period of time, expecting that you would eventually marry and then "the love of your life" walked out on you.

You may have felt the pain of rejection from your children, after having given them life and spent your life caring for and providing for them.

You may have experienced the extreme rejection that comes through divorce or death.

Every one of us have been victims of rejection in one form or another. Rejection is a painful experience no matter what the cause, but too often we begin to agree with the "rejecter's" opinion of us. This can cause you to carry a feeling of inferiority or of being "not quite good enough" all of your life.

Some people defend against rejection by learning to compete and by scheming to get ahead in order to be accepted. These people strive for significance through their performance, so they are prone to the added strongholds of perfectionism, anxiety, and stress. Yielding control to God is difficult for them because control and manipulation of people and circumstances have been their survival skills.

Others pursue the impossible goal of avoiding rejection by learning to be a "people pleaser," continually working to satisfy friends and family members by being helpful and encouraging. The problem is that when the inevitable rejection still comes, it reinforces their belief that they really are unlovable and that something must indeed be wrong with them.

Then there are the rebels who say, "I don't need your love. In fact, I don't need anyone, including God." Deep inside they still crave acceptance, but they refuse to acknowledge their need. They will often dress and behave in ways intended to alienate and push people away. Rebels are marked by self-hatred and bitterness. They are often irresponsible and undisciplined.

Only by the supernatural power of God and the love of Jesus can we be truly healed of the residue from rejection. Remember, Jesus experienced total rejection. There was no sin, no personality or character flaw in Him that caused Him to be rejected. He was perfect. Yet He suffered undeserved rejection all of His life. He was rejected by His peers, by His family, and by the world He created. He even experienced rejection by God for us. Matthew 27:46 says, *"And about the ninth hour Jesus cried out with a loud voice, saying, 'Eli, Eli, lama sabachthani?' that is, 'My God, My God, why hast Thou forsaken Me?'"*

Jesus knows how rejection makes you feel. He has been there. He will comfort you, give you value, and restore your sense of who you are. When you give up your expectations of how you want to be treated and shift your focus to God's acceptance of you the curse of rejection will be reversed. Don't give any person who rejects you permission to put a price tag on you. God has put His price tag on you. You are worth so much that He gave Himself to die for you.

By the way, rejection is a two way street. When you are tempted to criticize or to reject others, think again.

Prison Cell #3: CONTROL

Most of us are masters at contributing to our own turmoil when we try to control either people or circumstances. Being in control is a human way of feeling secure, but it is a false security. Sometimes we fall into some type of control trap as an outgrowth of fear, insecurity, or a lack of self-esteem. The more secure you are, the less you will feel the need to control.

There are many open doors into the control trap. You may have had a dysfunctional authority over you. You may have been forced into an adult role due to an adult's addiction or a caregiver's mismanaging of the family finances. You may have been raised to believe that it's your job to take on the burden of your world. Your extended family, friends, spouse, and children may all believe that no matter what they do, you'll be there to fix things.

God has called us not to control, but to trust Him. He wants to set you free from the lie that you are responsible for the outcome of the lives around you.

Questions regarding control:

1. When circumstances are out of your control or when people are doing things you don't like, do you sense something rising up inside, wanting to "take charge" and straighten things out?
2. When things are not going your way, is your initial emotional response one of fear, anger, or a sense of shame (*I must have done something wrong to cause this problem.*)?
3. Do you ever use "spiritual performance" to try to influence others' opinions of you? Or to influence the outcome of a particular situation?
4. Do you look for "new, improved spiritual formulas" that will give you more leverage with God, trying to influence Him to answer more of your prayers?
5. Do you ever hear yourself thinking or saying, "I guess it's all up to me. If I don't do it, it won't get done"?
6. Do you ever overstep the bounds of your authority at home or at work?
7. Do you have difficulty adjusting to change?
8. When riding in the passenger seat of a car, do you tend to give directions?
9. Do you use manipulative behaviors such as tears, blame, or guilt trips to get your way?

If you answered "yes" to any of these questions, your next step toward freedom is to identify the source of your particular control issues.

Roots of control:

Fear: 2 Timothy 1:7 says, (KJV) *"For God hath not given us the spirit of fear; but of power, and of love, and of a sound mind."* Fear can be a natural response or an in-born pattern of your nervous system. Fear is usually learned from overanxious, worrying, or fearful parents. Fear can even affect your body physically in the form of anxiety attacks. The stress that comes when you try to control your relationships may cause you to drive people away and will ultimately steal your joy. You can become free of that stress by releasing your relationships to God and asking Jesus to take away the fear.

Anger: Ephesians 4:26-27 says, *"Be angry, and yet do not sin; do not let the sun go down on your anger, and do not give the devil an opportunity."* Anger is a strong emotion that will make a quick impression on someone else's spirit. But using your anger on others to manipulate them into doing what you want is sin, even though there may be a short-term reward for your emotional outbursts.

Shame: Genesis 3:7 says, *"Then the eyes of both of them were opened, and they knew that they were naked; and they sewed fig leaves together and made themselves loin coverings."* A person who feels shamed will have a tendency to control that is motivated by their need for predictability, safety, and respect. Shame has the effect of making you feel exposed and shown to be flawed or unworthy. A false face is formed and the real you goes into hiding. After years of this, the layers of defense and pretense are so intense that you lose sight of who you really are. One of the ways shame manifests itself as control is through perfectionism. Anyone who feels there is something imperfect about them will try to hide behind an attempt to do everything perfectly. Along with this perfectionism comes a haunting fear of failure.

Have you ever found yourself in any of these "direct control" roles?

1. The Boss is an obvious controller.
2. The Mother is always scolding or pampering people.
3. The Nag has a devastating effect, like a gnawing on the soul. Nagging can spiritually and emotionally strip the inner strength and identity of the one being verbally assaulted.
4. The Intimidator likes to instill fear with cautions, veiled threats, and hints of rejections. It is stressful for everyone living under this type of control. An intimidated spouse may become sneaky or secretive to avoid the Intimidator's wrath.

Many choose to control in more subtle and deceptive ways in order not to be viewed as aggressive or controlling. Indirect control can actually be more detrimental than direct control because it disguises true motives. Most people cannot be pushed to do something they don't want to do, especially by their spouses, so they resort to forms of indirect control because at first it appears to yield the desired results. This type of control creates confusion, frustration, and, eventually, hatred.

Have you ever found yourself in any of these "indirect control" roles?

1. The Manipulator will use tears or sexual favors to get their way.
2. The Martyr appears to be self-sacrificing, but controls through guilt and obligation. This person usually suffers from a poor self-image.
3. The Invalid sees that being sick is not so bad when it gives them more power and attention and relieves them of responsibilities they don't want to fulfill.
4. The Mask is overly sweet and accommodating until they don't get their way. Then the mask comes off and beneath the sweet exterior is a very angry person.
5. The Flirt exerts control by acting cute, playful, and teasing. They project being happy and outgoing when they are really unhappy and frightened.
6. The Belittler finds subtle ways to belittle a spouse or co-worker, often with humor ("just kidding") or admiration of what other people have.

By now you've probably identified more than one stronghold that has been holding you prisoner. It may seem that the ground that once felt so secure under you is being dug up right beneath your feet. The paths you once walked may now seem cluttered with lies and self-defeating behaviors. Your prison doors are being shaken. You may have been comfortable with your old way of doing things, but God wants to release you from all your issues, setting you free to be all He has called you to be.

Chapter 11

God's Escape Plan

II Corinthians 10:3-6 says:

"For though we walk in the flesh, we do not war according to the flesh, for the weapons of our warfare are not of the flesh, but divinely powerful for the destruction of fortresses. We are destroying speculations and every lofty thing raised up against the knowledge of God, and we are taking every thought captive to the obedience of Christ, and we are ready to punish all disobedience, whenever your obedience is complete."

God has provided a way of escape from every type of stronghold. The key to unlocking the prison door is to control the thoughts in your mind before they control you. Since some of your strongholds originated as thoughts raised up against the knowledge of God, learning to know God as a loving Father and yourself as His accepted child is your starting place. You're not just up against the world and the flesh. You're also up against the devil who is scheming to fill your mind with thoughts which are opposed to God's plan for you.

Once any thought becomes a habit, a tormenting emotion, or an irrational "obsessive-compulsive" behavior, human effort is useless in tearing it down. At that point, no amount of discipline or determination will be successful long-term because satanic strongholds require divine demolition. Only God can provide the *dudimas* dynamite power necessary to destroy a stronghold. Remember, Satan's power lies only in his ability to deceive you, and his most effective deceptions are based on partial truths. Once you learn the Truth and how to use it, Satan loses his hold on you in that area. When you sense a struggle, increase your prayer time and time in God's word to keep Truth before your mind's eye. Allow new meditations to dwell in your heart by faith because your life will ultimately follow the direction of your thinking.

In order to win the battle for your mind, you need a strategy. If the strongholds in your mind are the result of conditioning, then you can be reconditioned by the renewing of your mind. Anything that has been learned can be unlearned. Romans 12:2 says, *"And do not be conformed to this world, but be transformed by the renewing of your mind, that you may prove what the will of God is, that which is good and acceptable and perfect."*

Strategic spiritual warfare means pursuing intimacy with Christ and lining yourself up with His purposes. You will be set free when you receive a personal word of Truth directly from the Source of Truth. The lie and its power over you will be gone. You will be free to live in that new truth. Then you must allow the perfect work Jesus began in your Spirit at your new birth to be worked out in your soul. Remember, if you could overcome on your own you wouldn't need Jesus.

We are commanded in Ephesians 6:10: *"Finally, be strong in the Lord, and in the strength of His might."* One of the strongest and most effective biblical methods that God has given you to increase your faith is the *fasting prayer.* Jesus demonstrated that there are areas of victory that will never be realized except through prayer combined with fasting. Matthew 6:17 says, *"But you, when you fast, anoint your head, and wash your face...."* Actually, Jesus does not even ask us to fast. He tells us. He did not say *if* you fast, but *when* you fast. There is no power in fasting other than the obedient yielding of yourself to God so that Jesus can flow through you in power and authority. Isaiah 58 is one of the best sources of information on fasting. First, verses 3-5 tell you how *not* to fast. Then the remaining verses instruct you on how to fast and on the benefits of fasting. The motive for fasting must be a heart full of love for God and the desire to be free. Look at the results promised in verse 6:

God will loose the bands of wickedness.
He will undo the heavy burdens.
The oppressed will go free.
Every yoke will be broken.

As we move closer to the end of the age, the pressures and the calamities of everyday life will increase. We are warned about the devil's end-time activities in Daniel 7:25: *"And he will speak out against the Most High and wear down the saints of the Highest One, and he will intend to make alterations in times and in law; and they will be given into his hand for a time, times, and half a time."* Many Christians on the front lines are already weary. Others have been "just going through the motions" for some time now. This is a confirmation of Daniel's warning that the enemy would try to wear out the saints and then deceive them. His ultimate goal is to thwart God's plan and God's timing for your destiny.

If you desire an increased anointing and for signs and wonders to follow you, you need to be sure that all three enemies of God -- the flesh, the world, and the devil -- are overcome in your life. Jesus overcame all three on the Cross. Now the degree to which you overcome them will be the degree to which Jesus can live His life through you.

Remember when Jesus was fasting and being tempted in the wilderness He kept silencing the enemy with the word *"It is written... It is written."* Finally, when the enemy saw that he could not deceive Jesus, Luke 4:13 tells us, *"And when the devil had finished every temptation, he departed from Him until an opportune time."*

In the Greek the word for "opportune time" is *kairos*. Satan knew that if he was ever going to stop Jesus' earthly ministry it had to be in that wilderness, and he used every weapon at his disposal. Jesus went into that forty day fast "full of the Holy Spirit," but Luke 4:14 says, *"And Jesus returned to Galilee in the power of the Spirit; and news about Him spread through all the surrounding district."* He came out not only full but *"in the power of the Holy Spirit"* and then began to heal the sick, raise the dead, and cause blinded eyes to see.

Just as they were with Jesus, Satan's target points are the *kairos* seasons in your life. These times provide windows of opportunity when you must win your battles and gain your victory by using the Word of God to silence and repel the enemy.

146

Once you make the decision to be free, God will make the provision for you to do anything He asks you to do. Once you recognize the sin involved in your stronghold and ask forgiveness, you will begin to see the lies used to construct and strengthen it. Tearing down the lies will begin to weaken the stronghold. Satan does not have the power or the authority to keep you in a prison of any kind of oppression, but he does try to deceive you into staying there.

Steps to Freedom

Let's review these steps to freedom.

1. Identify that you have a stronghold. Luke 11:21 says, *"When a strong man, fully armed, guards his own homestead, his possessions are undisturbed;"*
2. Confess your sin and ask forgiveness for opening the door to that oppression. Declare: "I want it closed, now!" and see it destroyed. Proverbs 18:12 says, *"Before destruction the heart of man is haughty, But humility goes before honor."*
3. Ask forgiveness for the sins of your parents.
4. Ask God to reveal every lie and replace them with Truth. Ask God to show you where your unbelief came in and how you can regain your freedom.
5. Begin to consistently bring every thought into submission to God's Word. II Corinthians 10:5 says, *"We are destroying speculations and every lofty thing raised up against the knowledge of God, and we are taking every thought captive to the obedience of Christ,"*

6. Guard you tongue because *your words can reopen the door!* James 3:5 says, *"So also the tongue is a small part of the body, and yet it boasts of great things. Behold, how great a forest is set aflame by such a small fire!"*
7. Be on guard against future deception.

Prayer:

Lord, I confess the sin of (anger, selfishness, pride, lust, or greed) that is out of my control. Please forgive me.
Cleanse me.
Create in me a new heart and renew a right spirit in me.
Lord, please remove from me the source that keeps this sin alive in me.
I reject the thought that I'll never change.
Holy Spirit, I ask You to replace the anger in my life with self-control and gentleness.
In Jesus' Name.

Rejection has been found to be one of the most difficult strongholds to break, so you may need to take even more drastic action if you still find yourself struggling in this area. First you must acknowledge the fact that you still have symptoms of rejection. Then each time that feeling comes begin to confess out loud who you are in Christ and that you are so loved by One Man that He was willing to die on a cross for you.

Prayer:

Lord, by the power of Your Word, I claim victory over rejection.

By the power of Your Word, destroy every word that has been spoken against me.
Lord, you have chosen me as Your child.
I know that Your love for me is unconditional and unchanging.
My own thoughts and feelings have been deceiving me.
I reject the lie of rejection that robs me of the joy of my inheritance as one accepted in the Beloved.
I speak to the mountains of self-doubt, fear of rejection, and inferiority, and break their power over my mind and emotions.
In Jesus' Name.

Continue to stand in faith and realize that deliverance will require a repetitive, ongoing process of cleansing and healing the hurts and the lies that have been planted in you throughout your lifetime. Go to God in prayer and ask Him to reveal the truth in each situation that brings you pain. Continue to confess the truth and to think on God's thoughts rather than on the thoughts of rejection. Strongholds that have paralyzed you for years can and will be broken as you continue to speak what God says about you.

Look at Ephesians 1:3-14 to see how special you are to God. You are blessed, chosen, loved, predestined, adopted, redeemed, forgiven, lavished with grace, included with Christ, sealed with the Spirit, and guaranteed an inheritance.

Remember that the Lord planned your life and formed you in your mother's womb. Psalm 139:16 says, *"Thine eyes have seen my unformed substance; And in Thy book they were all written, The days that were ordained for me, When as yet there was not one of them.*" He knows all about you and has chosen you. Psalm 56:8 says, *"Thou hast taken account of my wanderings; Put my tears in Thy bottle; Are they not in Thy book?"* and John 15:19 says, *"If you were of the world, the world would love its own; but because you are not of the world, but I chose you out of the world, therefore the world hates you."*

He loved you so much He died for you. John 3:16 says, *"For God so loved the world, that He gave His only begotten Son, that whoever believes in Him should not perish, but have eternal life."*

He has called you to be and to do something wonderful and unique. II Timothy 1:9 says, *"who has saved us, and called us with a holy calling, not according to our works, but according to His own purpose and grace which was granted us in Christ Jesus from all eternity."*

Focusing on these things doesn't mean you won't ever feel resentment at unfair treatment. It doesn't even take away the gnawing, empty sense of loss when someone doesn't value you or want to be with you as much as you value them. But don't overlook God's blessings just because there is something you don't have. Concentrating on what you've lost blinds you to all you've been given, and prevents you from receiving all that God has for your future. When Jesus opens the prison door, it's up to you to walk out.

You are now ready to walk the path from where you are to a much deeper, more gratifying level of intimacy with Jesus Christ. Until you are less vulnerable, continue to flood your mind with Truth. Remember, if you stray either consciously or unconsciously into Satan's area of operation, you can expect to be attacked one way or another. You can't continue to sin and win. If the enemy can get you to go back into bondage, the breakthrough or the inheritance will be lost or at least delayed until a future time. You must use radical caution when escaping from a stronghold.

Genuine healing and deliverance is divine. The key to experiencing real peace is in understanding that it is primarily an internal blessing. Peace with God is something every born again believer should already have. Romans 5:1 promises: *"Therefore having been justified by faith, we have peace with God through our Lord Jesus Christ."* It's not something you work up. It's something you received when you were born again. You can't control your external world, but you can control the inner world of your thoughts and emotions by allowing the peace of God to rule in your heart on a daily basis.

True freedom from a stronghold is *not* in *changing what happened in your past,* but in *interpreting* it from God's point of view and in the light of His Word. Struggling to maintain your peace or having to fight for a little joy will no longer be a problem to you unless you deliberately go against the truth and the new freedom Christ has given you. There may be chaos all around you, but your God is bigger than any crisis or catastrophe that you may have to face.

The Lord is issuing an urgent summons to prayer and fasting and loving one another. The enemy knows that your season is due and he's going about as a roaring lion seeking whom he may devour, trying to wear you out and to get you to run and hide in your emotional cave or to retreat back into your old ways of thinking and reacting. Your God says, "If you will go into the secret place and pray, I will listen. If you call upon Me, I will answer. If you search for me with all your heart, you will find Me."

Strength and breakthrough are within your reach in the Spirit if you are willing to pay the price for power through prayer and fasting and if you will worship God in Spirit and in truth. God is calling out a group of extraordinary people with extraordinary faith. He is saying, "If you will press into intense worship and intercession, I will enable you to see past the deceptions and to see through the confusion that surrounds you."

Matthew 5:8 says, *"Blessed are the pure in heart, for they shall see God."* The purity that attracts the attention of God comes from allowing Him to show us what is clogging or hindering His flow of life to us. Being able to live in this place requires spending the quality and quantity of time in the Lord's presence that allows your spirit to literally hide itself in God. You must learn to move with, not against, the promptings of the Holy Spirit. The anointing and the purity of your thoughts and motives will increase as you pursue Him as passionately as He has been pursuing you.

Miraculous signs, wonders, and provision are about to be released. Your opportunity to participate in this end-time move of God is contingent upon how you respond while the window of opportunity is open to come into the Presence of the Lord. God is asking you to count the cost and make a choice. Your time is now. Are you ready? Are you ready to see where God wants to take you from here? If you have dealt with the strongholds in your life, you are now like a rocket on the launching pad, ready to be propelled into your destiny. Let go of the past and allow fresh intimacy with God to launch His glorious plan for your future.

Prayer:

Lord, though this place is familiar, help me to trust You as You lead me to a better place.
Show me the way I must take to find Your joy.
As I determine to obey Your voice, honor me with restoration and healing.
Visit me, talk to me, help me to begin again.
I want to be a beautiful temple where You are happy to be.
Lord, I want to stop struggling against Your love and yield to You.
I know that I've settled for less than You intended for me.
You are more than able to release me from my past. Why should I cling to it?
Help me to discern what people, places, and things I should leave behind.
Break off the chains that bind me as I worship You.
Help me to realize that the Blood of Jesus shed on Calvary is enough to change me from the inside out and that my future doesn't have to be determined by my past.
Make my passion for You and Your Word so strong that it drives out all desires that aren't of You.
Teach me to love the things that You love and to hate the things that You hate.
I am weary and worn out.
I'm no longer interested in doing Your job.
I come to You emptied of my own ideas and agendas.
Please help me just to "let go."
I've been circling the mountain long enough.
I know it's time to strike out for new territory.

Help me to learn to stand strong against adversity when it comes, even to use the trials to take me higher in You.
Lord, I stand open to Your correction and guidance.
Direct me toward Your peace and surround me in it.
Please honor my attempts to receive Your healing and restoration.
I give You my pride, my longing for love, my loneliness, my hopes and dreams.
Help Me to understand that loss sometimes saves me from even greater pain.
In Jesus' Name.

DECLARATION OF TRUTH

My past is redeemed.
My faith is renewed.
My future is secure.
Now that I am free,
I refuse to look back, let up,
slow down, back away, or be still.
I no longer have to be right, first, praised, or rewarded.
I now live by faith, walk in power,
and am uplifted by prayer.
My mind is made up.
My heart is fixed.
My mission is clear.
I am more than a conqueror.

MORE ABOUT WOUNDED HEALERS

For too long the church has forced believers to deny their own emotional pain, insisting that the answer is to "Get over it!," "Let it go," or "Give it to God." This is not always possible without a helping hand when the pain is so real and the effects of it have taken such a toll spiritually, mentally, emotionally, and physically.

In the *Wounded Healers Workshops* God has provided a safe environment designed to provide a time of self-encounter and strong but gentle words of instruction, correction, and direction according to John 8:32: (*NIV*) *"Then you will know the truth, and the truth will set you free."*

After one *Wounded Healers Workshop*, participants wrote:

> "Thank you for having me at the *Wounded Healers* weekend. It was the biggest blessing in a two-fold manner for me. On a spiritual level, there were great truths in the teachings and honesty that touched my heart in ways I thought were gone for good. God in His infinite mercy is replacing a stony heart, a guarded heart, and reopening it to His presence and love. The weekend was and continues to be an eye-opening experience and a river of changes. My husband said my eyes were sparkling when I got home."

"The *Wounded Healers* weekend is a life-changing experience. Everyone who can attend SHOULD! The Wounded Healers manual is a "must have" for keeping you refreshed and empowering you for the rest of your life. Also the tapes and booklets offered are great! Thanks for such a blessed weekend!"

"I attended this weekend not knowing exactly what to expect, but I knew that I wanted all God had for me. It was so powerful. I have never been as physically affected by God's presence as I was that Saturday. My body could hardly contain the touch from 'The Man of Fire.' I knew as I left that weekend I knew I would never again be the same."

If you would like free information on how you can experience this life-changing encounter with truth or if you would like to invite Paula Russell to speak at your church or event, simply write or e-mail us.

Wounded Healers
P.O. Box 72201
Newport, Kentucky 41071

phone: 859-466-8827
email: spiritualhospital@yahoo.com

This book and other books, workbooks, tapes, and CD's by Paula Russell are available for purchase on our website:

www.woundedhealers.us